FOLLOWERS OF THE WAY

Followers of the Way

ॐ

By CARL J. SCHERZER

ॐ

THE CHRISTIAN EDUCATION PRESS
PHILADELPHIA

Library of Congress Catalog Card Number: 55-6521

Contents

How Old Are You?

And Pharaoh said to Jacob, "How many are the days of
the years of your life?"   —GENESIS 47:8

⋖§ "How old are you?" If you ask a little child that question, she may hold up three or four fingers to indicate the
number of years in her short lifetime. A small child does
not mind telling how old he is. Elderly people are usually
proud to tell their age, too, especially when they are beyond 85.

If you say to a middle-aged man, "How old are you?" he
may answer jokingly, "Jack Benny and I are 39." Or he
may reply, "Let me see, now. I will be 46, I think, on my
next birthday." Doubtless he is telling the approximate
truth, for you notice he says, "I think." Or, his reaction may
be, "I'm not ashamed of my age. I'm 46 and proud of it!
How old are you?"

If you ask a middle-aged woman how old she is, very
likely she will counter your question with one of her own,
"How old do you think I am?" If you prize discretion more
than honesty, you will subtract ten years from the age you
guess her to be, and she will love you for it. But if you value
honesty above all else, tell her your actual guess, and—"Well,
it was nice knowing you!" It would have been wiser not to
have asked the question in the first place.

Many people are sensitive about their age, often with good
reason. But actually a person's true age can never be reck-
oned in years. Many old people are young in their attitudes,
while some young people are old in their thoughts and
ways. "You are only as old as you think you are," as the old
saying goes.

When Joseph introduced Jacob, his father, to Pharaoh, the ruler of the Egyptians, the old patriarch blessed the monarch. Pharaoh, searching for something to say in reply, blurted out the question, "How old are you?" Jacob's reply shows his attitude toward the years. "I am 130 years old," he said, "and have mostly enjoyed them. But so far as years are concerned, some of my ancestors lived longer than I."

Years are like good health. They are important to us only in so far as we can use them well. There is no special merit merely in living a long time—some other creatures on earth have a life span far longer than that of man. The important thing is what we do with the years it pleases God to give us.

Hampering Fears

> After these things the word of the Lord came to Abram in a vision, "Fear not, Abram, I am your shield; your reward shall be very great."
> —GENESIS 15:1

This promise of God was the only reassurance Abram had beyond his own resources when he left his homeland to venture into an unfamiliar country. It required a lot of courage on Abram's part to go, with all his possessions, from a place where he was well known, from the land he had inherited from his father, to settle in another place, far away. With the assurance of God's presence, he had sufficient courage to undertake this adventurous mission.

Many people are hampered by fears, especially the fear of adventure. Dr. G. Ernest Thomas in his excellent book,

Faith Can Master Fear, tells of an incident at a wedding reception. A bachelor uncle congratulated the bride and groom by saying, "So you're going to live in one room and both work." "Yes, we are," replied the bride. "We'll get along somehow!"

Then the uncle became wistful, although the wedding couple were too absorbed in their own happiness to notice. He told the young people that when he was young and in love his wages were small and he saw little opportunity for advancement in his work. He had missed his chance for happiness with the girl he loved because he was afraid of an uncertain future.

I had opportunity to counsel with a group of high school seniors who indicated their interest in entering the ministry. When I advised these young people that they would need to study for four more years in an accredited college and then to enroll for three more years of study in a theological seminary, I noticed expressions of disappointment on some of their faces.

Some of these young people will change their minds about entering the ministry now that they know how much preparation precedes ordination. If any young person is afraid to pay the price, however, it may be just as well for him to pursue another calling, because our Lord wants young men and young women who have sufficient faith in him to overcome their fears. The old saying, "Nothing ventured, nothing gained," applies to the spiritual and mental phases of life as well as the physical.

One of the best ways to dispel fear in connection with any adventure is to rely upon God. God is not an impersonal Creator of the universe; he is an almighty Father, who loves each one of his children. With the assurance of his interest

in us we can find the necessary courage to venture into unfamiliar countries. All we need is the certainty that our aims
conform to his will for our lives.

Aiming in the Right Direction

> But a certain man drew his bow at a venture, and struck the
> king of Israel between the scale armor and the breastplate;
> therefore he said to the driver of his chariot, "Turn about,
> and carry me out of the battle, for I am wounded."
>
> —I KINGS 22:34

◆§ This young man who drew his bow at a venture was
not a trained soldier. Evidently he was a farm boy who
enlisted in the army because his friends urged him to. Then
when he found himself in the midst of veteran soldiers, he
became the object of many jokes. The veterans laughed
when they watched him try to handle a bow and arrow,
because he had no training for it.

Every one of the country boy's comrades wanted the honor
of wounding or capturing the enemy's king. No one, including the lad himself, suspected that he would accom-
plish quite accidentally what they were all intent on doing,
for he was so unskilled with the bow. All that he did was to
aim his arrow in the right direction, pull the bow taut, close
his eyes, and let the arrow fly.

Unfortunately for the king of Israel, the boy's arrow pene-
trated his body between the joints of his armor, inflicting a
fatal wound. When the king was carried from his chariot,
the boy from the farm was acclaimed a hero.

Aiming in the right direction is the essential first step in the accomplishment of any goal. Through the escape of wishful thinking it is all too easy to imagine ourselves as having succeeded in any task we may want to undertake. But there is a big difference between wishing and accomplishing. If the wish directs us to devote our talents and energies to the task, then it serves the wholesome purpose of turning our aim in the right direction.

Aim is important in wholesome living. Some parents believe that they should not influence their children in the matter of religious ideals. "When he is old enough, he can decide for himself what church he wants to attend," they will say. In the meantime, during the formative years of his life the child receives little or no religious direction, and when he is "old enough" to make a decision he has no background of experience to guide him.

The time to start aiming in the right direction is always the present in the life of any individual regardless of age. Psychologists say, however, that the direction of a child's life is determined by his first six years. Study the lives of the happy and contented people you know and you will find that many of them owe their success in the art of living to wise parents, teachers, and pastors who taught them early to aim in the right direction.

Sunglasses

The eye is the lamp of the body. So, if your eye is sound, your whole body will be full of light; but if your eye is not sound, your whole body will be full of darkness. If then the light in you is darkness, how great is the darkness!

—MATTHEW 6:22, 23

◆§ During the summer months when the glare of the sun is at its height we like to wear sunglasses. The colored lenses soften the dazzling rays and keep us from squinting. At the same time these glasses color the scenes around us according to the tint of the lenses. If the lenses in our glasses happen to be blue, then everything we see through them will appear blue also. Driving over the highway on a bright afternoon, even the blue sky with its white fleecy clouds looks ominous, as if a storm were continually threatening.

There is a psychological truth here. When we view things through the dark glasses of a critical attitude we can always find something wrong. Some people seem to be continually looking for the unpleasant. They go to a party convinced ahead of time that they will have a boring evening—and they do!

Looking through dark, critical glasses, such people find many things to criticize. A farmer who was wont to look through dark glasses happened to meet a friend immediately after a refreshing shower. No rain had fallen for a long time, and the earth was parched. Then the shower came to save the growing crops. The friend, happy over the break in the drought, exclaimed, "What a nice rain that was and how we needed it!" To which the farmer retorted, "Well—yes, I guess it was. But it soaked right in!" Instead of being

6

thankful for the refreshing rain he complained because it soaked into the earth!

The tint of the glasses determines the beauty of the landscape. If we look through the glasses of love, things appear beautiful. If they did not, there would be many more unmarried people. Whether love is blind as they say, we cannot be sure, but we do know that anyone whom we love seems beautiful to us. Looked at through the dark glasses of jealousy even the most lovable person can appear ugly. The red lenses of anger likewise distort the appearance of one toward whom we direct our rage. Only when the red glasses are removed do we see the person as he really is.

Our Lord had such instances in mind when he told his hearers that the light of the body is the eye. If we look for evil and delight in it, then our days will be filled with darkness, but if our eyes look out through lenses tinted with Christian love, then our lives will be full of light. We usually see what we really want to see.

Growing Over the Wall

> Joseph is a fruitful bough, a fruitful bough by a spring; his branches run over the wall. —GENESIS 49:22

A clean white picket fence clearly defined the limits of the front yard. But the authority of the children whose front yard it was, was not recognized by their playmates beyond the fence. There was a spreading plum tree in the front of the yard on the side of the house. Its branches, filled with

7

delicious plums at the peak of ripeness, reached far out over the white fence. When the plums were at their juiciest, the question arose in the minds of all of the children: To whom did the plums on the outside of the fence belong? The children on the inside felt that they belonged to them because the tree was on their side of the fence. Their playmates also claimed them because they grew outside the yard.

The mother of the house overheard her children quarreling about the plums. Calling her youngsters into the house, she suggested that since they already had more than their share of the fruit, they could easily afford to share with their companions. Once the children agreed to this suggestion they stopped quarreling. More than that, they learned the joy of being unselfish, for the other children loved them for their kindness. In time they found more pleasure in the plums they shared than in those they kept for themselves.

In the book of Genesis Joseph is compared to a fruitful bough of a tree growing by a desert well, with branches running over the wall. Joseph was generous and outgoing, and shared his life and his possessions with others. Risen to a position of wealth and influence in Egypt, Joseph might well have forgotten his father and his brothers. His brothers had mistreated him, selling him into slavery. Many another person under similar circumstances would have nourished a lifelong hatred for his kin. But Joseph realized that God had turned what was apparently a misfortune into a blessing for him. Joseph wanted to share his prosperity with his family, and it was for that reason that he first tested his brothers' integrity and then provided the means for them and their old father, Jacob, to come and settle on fertile soil.

So it is in every life. There is a story of a minister in Scotland whose parsonage yard was enclosed by a wall of stone which prevented passersby from enjoying the flowers which the clergyman tended with great care. To overcome this hindrance, each day he cut a bouquet of his most beautiful blossoms and placed them outside the wall in an urn for everyone to enjoy. He appreciated most of all the flowers he shared with others.

Sharing is the essence of the Christian way of life. The branches of our tree of life flourish as we mature in our faith until they hang over the fence and produce fruit which can be shared with others. "You will know them by their fruits" (Matthew 7:16).

What Have You?

One of his diciples, Andrew, Simon Peter's brother, said to him, "There is a lad here who has five barley loaves and two fish; but what are they among so many?"

—JOHN 6:8, 9

◂§ It happened in a large gathering, a crowd estimated at five thousand people. They were so much interested in what Jesus told them that they did not notice the passing of time. Then when he finished speaking, they were hungry, and Jesus was aware of their need.

Jesus was always concerned about the physical welfare of people, and this situation was no exception. When the disciples saw that he wanted to provide food for the crowd, one of them, Philip, offered the discouraging opinion that it would require 200 pennies-worth of bread to feed them.

He knew the disciples did not have that much money among them.

Another disciple, Andrew, also wanted to help, but, like Philip, did not know what to do. In the crowd he had noticed a lad who had five barley loaves and two small fish. He called this to Jesus' attention—not that he felt it would help very much.

The disciples must have been as much surprised as the lad when Jesus motioned for him. The boy had never dreamed that the great Teacher would even notice him. So, it was with eagerness that he followed the summons. When Jesus asked for the bread and the fish, the lad gave them gladly, happy because he had something which the great Teacher could use.

The rest is familiar. To the astonishment of everyone there, Jesus used the loaves of bread and the two small fish, multiplying them until there was sufficient food for all. When the remnants were gathered, after all had eaten, they filled twelve baskets!

A man once said to his pastor, "If only I were rich I would make a substantial donation to the new church, but right now I can't do anything." There are many other people like this man, waiting until they get rich to do something for their Lord. The lad in the story was a poor boy with only a few fish and a few loaves of bread, but he was willing to give them to Jesus. When he did, they were used wonderfully, illustrating the truth that anything that is dedicated to our Lord becomes infinitely more precious the moment the possessor says, "This I give thee, Lord. Let it be used now in thy service!"

Think a moment. What have you that you are willing to dedicate to your Lord? Strength? Musical talent? Teaching ability? A fluent tongue? A little money? Some used clothing that is still good? Take an inventory and see if there isn't something you have that your Lord can use. As it was with Andrew and the lad, you too may be surprised with the wonderful way your Lord can use what you dedicate to him.

Making Friends

But I have called you friends.   —JOHN 15:15

❧ Sarah was a wallflower. Her mother almost had to force her to attend youth meetings at the church, or social gatherings sponsored by her school. She complained bitterly to her pastor that other people were not friendly to her, mentioning especially the youth group of the church. "It's run by a clique," she lamented. "If you aren't in the clique, no one pays any attention to you. That's why I don't like to come."

Sarah's pastor looked at her appraisingly, trying to understand why she felt so left out. "Her appearance is rather plain," he thought to himself, "but she could improve that considerably with a little care. No, the trouble is deeper than that. Somewhere along the way she has acquired feelings of inferiority which lead her to withdraw from others. In a crowd she is afraid and gets flustered when people try to talk to her. It is only when some members of the group coax her that she enters into the games and the fun. No wonder that after a while her companions get the impression that she doesn't want to be with them. Naturally they get tired of coaxing, and let her alone.

"Sarah is old enough now to learn that the way to have friends is to be a friend," the pastor said to himself. "Instead of blaming others she needs to be helped to find ways to contribute her share to the companionship and the fun."

In the same youth group at the church was a girl named Lucille. Lucille was potentially not nearly so good-looking as Sarah, but her friendly attitude made her popular with the others. The minister talked confidentially with Lucille about Sarah's problem and asked her to help him. Between them they managed to give Sarah some responsibilities in the youth organization, asking for her opinion on matters of policy, and trying in other ways to restore her confidence in herself. Before she knew what was happening to her, Sarah was not only accepted, but actually liked by the group.

The way to have friends is to be a friend, yet each of us has one friend who is always available. He is Jesus Christ, our Savior. We need never fear that he will let us down when we need a friend most. At the same time the truth of our story holds good here, too. If we want him for our companion we can merit his friendship by being a friend to him.

Be Angry!

Be angry but do not sin.   —EPHESIANS 4:26

•§ Many people believe that it is always wrong to be angry. Those who hold that view do not make a distinction between

12

anger over an injustice and losing control of one's temper. The Apostle Paul certainly would not urge people to lose their tempers, but he does affirm that there is a way to be angry which is not sinful.

When Abraham Lincoln was a young man he made a trip to New Orleans by flatboat. Newly arrived, he had walked only a short distance from the docks when he came upon a sight such as he had never seen before. Some auctioneers were selling Negroes as slaves to the highest bidders. Many of the buyers thought of these black people as they thought of their horses and cows. The sight of such cruelty outraged Lincoln's sense of decency because he rebelled at the idea that any human being could feel that he had the right to buy or sell any other human being. Anger caused him to make up his mind to do everything he could to abolish such a sinful practice. He never forgot that scene in New Orleans. When the opportunity finally came, he used his authority and influence as President of the United States to abolish slavery.

The best example of a holy anger was presented by our Lord when he drove the money-changers from the temple. These wicked men were overcharging, cheating, and otherwise duping sincere worshipers who came to the temple for the purpose of making sacrifices. Such a practice Jesus could not condone. He expressed his anger by forceful and effective action.

When an individual becomes so tolerant that he either condones or overlooks almost anything that is wrong, then he is so good that he is in danger of becoming good for nothing. Crime, lust, racial prejudice, religious bigotry— these are some of the sins that should arouse the anger of any Christian who has convictions. Unless there are people who have the courage to become angry enough to oppose sinful practices and attitudes, we can make no progress in improving human relations.

A Nation's Greatness

> Where there is no prophecy the people cast off restraint, but blessed is he who keeps the law. —PROVERBS 29:18

What makes a nation great? You need to travel only a limited distance in this country to be impressed with the beauty of the land and the bounty of its resources. A clergyman who went by plane from Evansville, Indiana to Atlanta, Georgia for a speaking engagement delights to talk about the trip. He was greatly impressed by the beauty of the country over which he flew that summer morning. He saw rich river valleys, farms with fields neatly arranged, cities with their tall buildings reaching into the sky, the rolling hills of Georgia covered with forests. As he saw this vast and beautiful land he thought to himself, "God has been very good to us who live in the United States. He has given us far more than we really deserve."

Does America's greatness lie in its valleys and hills, forests and mines, small towns and great cities? To some extent, yes, because all of these contribute to our abundant life. But other countries of the world are also richly blessed with such resources. Why do we believe that there is no country on earth like our own? We love it and we are grateful for the privilege of living here, but the reasons for our love and gratitude go far beyond America's physical and natural resources.

Our nation was founded on spiritual values. The colonists wanted to get away from the oppressions which curbed their economic, spiritual, and mental freedom. They dreamed of a land where people would be free under law, have equal opportunities, and be permitted to practice their religion as God guided them. They wanted to be rid of class distinctions, so prevalent in Europe at the time.

They succeeded in writing the principles of liberty into our Declaration of Independence, the Constitution and the laws, though not without opposition. There are always shortsighted people who want the liberty of their own convictions, but who feel that they are so right that they must deny others the freedom to disagree with them. One evidence of this spirit is religious bigotry. Our forefathers were wise enough to anticipate this danger and they took the positive path in guaranteeing liberty and justice for all. Today, ours is one of the few countries on earth whose citizens are assured that they have the right to life, liberty, and the pursuit of happiness.

Freedom, however, is not free. Only as long as we have the courage to uphold these ideals will we live in a free land. The promise of ease is the lure with which dictators bait their people. For promises of security people give up one freedom after another, until finally the state takes them over body and soul. Then they find that they have no liberty, no security, and no ease.

God has created us and made it possible for us to be his children. In the Sermon on the Mount Jesus points the way. It costs something to be a child of God but it is worth it to be able to say, "I am a freeborn child of God." When people are willing to exchange spiritual values for a promised security they have lost their vision. We love our country because here we may live with others who share our ideals and who are willing to sacrifice for them. That is the spirit that gives our country its true greatness.

Such As I Have

> But Peter said, "I have no silver and gold, but I give you what I have; in the name of Jesus Christ of Nazareth, walk."
> —THE ACTS 3:6

We are often asked to give to worthy enterprises and causes. The poor need our help; for their care local, state, and federal government has largely assumed responsibility. Aside from those who receive welfare aid of some form or another, there are many families who have such a small income that they cannot bear the burden of large expenditure that a sudden calamity may demand. In many cities there are clubs and organizations that aim to help people of this kind. In addition we have associations for the blind and for the crippled, church homes and hospitals, along with various state institutions. All of these are devoted to the care and nurture of less fortunate people.

Christ's spirit of compassion may be regarded as the source of all our modern humanitarian effort. There was very little, if any, organized philanthropy before the advent of Jesus. In his time beggars sat, hobbled along the street, or were carried to public places where they pleaded for help. Places of heavy traffic were chosen for that purpose; that is why a certain lame man was carried daily and placed at the gate of the temple which was called Beautiful. Here he appealed to Peter and John as they were going into the temple to pray.

To throw a surplus coin as an alms would have been the usual response, but Peter and John had no money to share with the poor man. Like many other benefactors of mankind they did have other things they could give. Florence Nightingale, William Shakespeare, Martin Luther, Abraham Lincoln, Booker T. Washington and other immortals had little silver and gold, but what they contributed to humanity was more important than the gifts of great philanthropists.

We do not regard disparagingly gifts of money which are given to worthy causes and needy individuals. In our economy the kingdom of God needs gold and silver as well as paper money and checks. Each should share proportionately as God has prospered him.

Peter and John had not even a widow's mite to share with the lame man, but they did not use this lack of funds as an excuse to ignore his plea. Halfway apologizing for their own poverty, Peter said, "I have no silver and gold, but I give you what I have." Then he called on the Lord to heal the man, took him by the hand, helped him arise in the name of the Lord, and the man was healed.

The lame man begged for a coin and received healing. Peter had no money to share, but he was willing to give what he could, and it turned out to be worth more than a silver coin. Many of us who have little money to give do have resources of love, ingenuity, strength, courage, or other talents. These we can share with our fellowmen if we desire. They are often needed just as badly as money, and usually they are much more helpful.

17

Where the Tree Grows

> He is like a tree planted by streams of water, that yields its fruit in its season, and its leaf does not wither. In all that he does, he prospers. —PSALM 1:3

◄§ Driving to the summit of one of the peaks in the Rocky Mountains, we noticed as we approached the timber line how twisted the pine trees were. At the timber line the pines were even more widely spaced—small, twisted, and gnarled by the fierce winds. Higher on the mountain peak there were no more trees. The climate was too much for them. The rocky earth could not feed them.

Those gnarled and twisted trees remind us of the soul that is overly exposed to the winds and the cold of sin. That soul is undernourished also and stands as a sad caricature of the tall, beautiful tree it might have been.

The psalmist observed that a tree which is in the proper environment and has good nourishment brings forth fruit in its season. If it is growing near a permanent supply of water its leaf does not wither and it grows profusely.

Psychologists and sociologists tell us that environment is a factor as important as heredity in human life. It is even believed that a person's intelligence quotient can be raised about ten per cent by favorable factors in his environment. The contrary is also true; a flower that struggles to grow by a coal mine will eventually shrivel from the coal dust.

Abraham Lincoln and Jefferson Davis were born a few hundred miles apart. Abraham Lincoln moved northward and the dust of the north fell on him. Jefferson Davis moved southward and the environment of the south influenced his life. Both were men of outstanding talents and ability. Environmental factors shaped the destinies of their lives.

For many of us the environment of God's Word provided by the Church is the determining factor in life and character. The soil from which the soul of man receives its nourishment is the Word of God. The water is the Spirit of God that comes into the life of the person who lives by the truths of the Bible. The fruit of the tree is Christian service that expresses itself in acts of kindness, consideration for others, fairness, and love.

Song in the Night

> But about midnight Paul and Silas were praying and singing hymns to God, and the prisoners were listening to them. —ACTS 16:25

A song in the night! Paul and Silas were in prison, with backs bleeding and their feet in stocks. They could have been downcast, feeling that God had forsaken them. But instead of complaining, they prayed and sang hymns! Perhaps the walls of that jail had never reverberated with the music of hymns. Those old stones were accustomed to curses, pleas for mercy, and cries for help. The jailer himself probably never heard anything like that before, and when the earthquake occurred about midnight he immediately thought of these two men who could sing in the night. He knew there was something unusual about them.

Christians have been singing in the night ever since, singing in the night of anxiety, grief, worry, sickness, pain, or calamity. Singing in the night is not like whistling in the dark. That is only an attempt to hide a fear. Singing in the night is made possible by the courage born of faith.

"This is the victory that overcomes the world, our faith." These words were written by one of the men who sang in prison. Paul and Silas were certain that God was with them. Just how he would help them they did not know, but they were absolutely certain that he would. That is why they were not surprised when the earthquake shook the building and their shackles were loosed.

It is such confidence in the power of God to help in a trying situation that enables us to sing in the night of trouble. We place ourselves in God's care, knowing that to them that love him all things work together for good.

"It was in the very early hours of the morning," a recuperating patient said, "that I heard the mockingbird. The doctor had told me I would have to submit to an operation, and it was hard to accept the news. During the night I rolled from one side to the other. I turned over and buried my face in the pillow. The house was so quiet I could hear the even breathing of my husband and of the two boys when they moved in their beds in the next room. I tried to relax, I prayed, and then in the stillness I heard a mockingbird in the tree outside my window. She was teaching her young one to sing. It made me feel better to know that they also were awake. How I wished I could be as carefree as they, singing before the dawn. 'Before the dawn,' I thought. 'That is it! The day is coming—light again. God will give me light again if I trust him enough.' Thinking such thoughts I fell asleep. When I awoke the sun was up, shining through the slats of my window shade. It was light again."

Refreshing Waters

> And Isaac dug again the wells of water which had been dug in the days of Abraham his father.   —GENESIS 26:18

◄§ When Abraham parted from Lot to settle in a new location, the first thing he did was to have wells dug. The water was necessary to nourish his flocks and his people.

When anything is so very precious, it becomes a vulnerable point of attack for an enemy. The Philistines did not want Abraham in that land. They knew how to make life impossible for him; they filled his wells with earth. Abraham had to move to another territory.

His son Isaac, who succeeded him as head of the family, decided to return to the land of his father because it promised greater production. The first thing he did upon arrival was to dig again the wells which they had dug in the days of Abraham.

In a measure these incidents parallel the history of our own country. Our forefathers came to America from various lands because wells there had become filled with earth. These wells, however, were of a spiritual nature. The founders of our country were tired of the eternal conflicts of Europe, the tyranny of rulers, and the suppression of religious freedom.

Having settled in this land they dug again the wells of freedom of expression, of conscience, and the exercise of true religion. The Bible became the symbol of their crusade for liberty in a new land. The refreshing waters flowed again and the wells were bequeathed to succeeding generations. There is always the danger of an enemy's attack at the most vulnerable spot, and many attempts have been made and are being made to fill our spiritual wells with earth.

The enemy need not necessarily be a foreign nation. The most vicious of all is the enemy who poses as a friend and at the same time attempts to fill our wells. The ideologies or philosophies which attempt to deny the value of spiritual forces are the Philistines of our day. They attack the most important well first of all, the Bible. The next step is to fill the well of the Church—to muzzle its prophets and finally to close its doors. Once that is done the rest becomes comparatively easy. One freedom after another is taken away until the people become the misguided slaves of a minority group that profits from the suppression.

We want to keep those wells open so that the waters can refresh human souls. It may mean digging again and again, but the results are worth more than any sacrifice that we may have to make. Has not someone said that the price of liberty is eternal vigilance?

Closer Than a Brother

> There are friends who pretend to be friends, but there is a friend who sticks closer than a brother. —PROVERBS 18:24

◆§ It is said of King Midas that he was granted the privilege of having his greatest desire satisfied, so he had to decide what it was that he wanted above everything else. At first glance it might seem to be very easy to express our greatest desire, but the more we think about it the more complex the problem becomes. King Midas evidently thought that he wanted money above all else. He was under the impression that with money he could buy anything he needed for his happiness. His great wish was that everything he touched would turn to gold.

He must have had a lot of fun for a little while, watching various objects turn to precious gold as he touched them with his magic fingers. But before long he found that he could get too much gold, especially when the time came to eat and when he wanted to touch a loved one. Then he realized there are many things in life that are much more valuable than gold and that his wish was a terrible mistake.

What if we were told that we could have our one great desire granted? What would that wish be? Solomon prayed for wisdom because he wanted it more than anything else. Some people would ask for money, others for success and honor. A few would request unlimited power over others, forgetting that power brings great responsibilities with it.

The wise man in Proverbs calls our attention to the great value of a friend, who, he says, "sticks closer than a brother." Friendship is important in life and a lonely person is usually very unhappy. Relatives can also be friends. Someone has said that we can choose our friends but that our relatives are wished upon us. This observation is unkind because our relatives may be our friends also; there is no reason why they cannot be both.

If we really want friends we can have them through the simple expedient of being friendly ourselves. A woman complained to her pastor about the members of the church, who, she said, were not friendly with her. "No one ever comes to see me," she whined. The truth was that she made herself hard to approach, was unpleasant in conversation, and usually made derogatory remarks about others. She certainly did not invite the friendship of others. Anyone who is pleasant and sincerely interested in others will have no trouble in making friends.

There is One above all others whose friendship we would cultivate. He is closer than a brother, for we can have him with us always, to share our thoughts and our hopes, our disappointments and our joys. With him in the heart we need never be lonely or afraid.

The First Word From the Cross

> And Jesus said, "Father, forgive them; for they know not what they do." —LUKE 23:34

It happened one Friday on a hill outside Jerusalem. There, at about nine o'clock in the morning, they nailed him on a cross between two thieves. At last his enemies were quite certain that they had disposed of him. So pleased were they with their achievement that they came out to the scene of the execution to gloat in satisfaction.

Members of the Sanhedrin, as well as scribes, Pharisees, and other officials milled through the crowd and sought the favor of the people by telling them that this was being done to protect them. The three crucified men, they said, were all trouble makers and proved criminals. They focused their venom on the one in the center. Individuals in the mob became so aroused that they hurled epithets at Jesus and challenged him to come down from the cross. In scorn they shouted that he claimed to help others and now he could not even help himself.

A few feet away from the cross, the Roman soldiers who were placed there decided to cast lots for Jesus' robe. According to custom such personal possessions of a criminal became the property of the executioners. They found that Jesus' garment was woven without a seam and to divide it among them would ruin it, so they decided to gamble for it. They were altogether unconcerned about the suffering of those whom they had crucified.

When Jesus looked down from the cross his eyes saw faces flashing anger at him. The one who had loved people so much was now almost alone in his distress. Almost alone! There were a few who had enough courage to face the disgrace of that moment. His mother was there, supported by John, the disciple, as well as her sister, Mary of Magdala, and another Mary who was the wife of Cleophas. With bowed heads they sobbed their sorrow. How pitifully few they were in comparison with the hating and shouting mob. Where now were the rest of the disciples, or the many whom he had healed or helped in one way or another? The latter, perhaps, knew nothing about this and therefore might be excused, but the disciples had been with him when he was arrested the previous night!

If anyone ever had reasons to be resentful, Jesus certainly did on Calvary that day. He had never shown hatred toward any person and had spent his life doing good. On many occasions he had taught his disciples the importance of love and forgiveness. Now upon the cross he witnessed to the truth of his teaching. When it seemed that surely hatred and jealousy had won the day, he prayed in a clear voice, "Father, forgive them; for they know not what they do."

In these words there is hope for a world in which so many are motivated by base impulses. Although it may seem at times that evil forces are ruling the affairs of man, amid the darkness we see a light when we hear the voice of Eternal Love saying, "Father, forgive them."

The Second Word

And he said to him, "Truly, I say to you, today you will be with me in Paradise." —LUKE 23:43

~§ The two criminals who were crucified on each side of Jesus heard the accusations and mockery of the crowd and so they learned that he claimed unusual powers. It is possible that either or both of them knew about him previously or even heard him speak, but the Scriptures do not mention that they did.

At first the one malefactor joined the mob in railing at Jesus and said, "Are you not the Christ? Save yourself and us!" The man on the other side was of a different sort. There are scholars who believe that these two criminals were companions previously. The subsequent expressions of the one indicate that he was reared in a God-fearing Hebrew home where his parents taught him the importance of goodness and discipline. But perhaps when he grew older the wrong crowd seemed more attractive. His parents tried to dissuade him, but he thought that he was big enough to take care of himself. As often happens in such cases, he chose as his ideal the ringleader of the crowd and thought it was smart to be associated with him. This fellow led him into one questionable episode after another as he went ever farther down the road to ultimate ruin.

Now, hanging on a cross, he could not avoid seeing Jesus as he looked toward his leader who had brought him to this horrible end. It must have been with utter disgust that he heard this braggart mock the man who had never harmed either of them. A few months before he would have joined his partner in the railery. Facing death this man whom he had idealized appeared in a different light, and for once he had enough courage to oppose him, saying, "Do you not fear God, since you are under the same sentence of condemnation? And we indeed justly; for we are receiving the due reward of our deeds; but this man has done nothing wrong."

Then he turned to Jesus and with a depth of contrition in his words, said, "Jesus, remember me when you come in your kingly power."

Jesus knew what was in his heart and here on Calvary yet once more he opened the doors of heaven to welcome a sincerely changed person. With the authority of the Son of God, Jesus answered, "Truly, I say to you, today you will be with me in Paradise."

This incident in the dying moments of Jesus' earthly life gives hope to all who are concerned about the eternal welfare of loved ones. The divine arms of mercy are always extended. Though it may require a drastic experience before we are induced to accept this mercy, the possibility of salvation is never withdrawn as long as we live.

The Third Word

> When Jesus saw his mother, and the disciples whom he loved standing near, he said to his mother, "Woman, behold your son!" Then he said to the disciple, "Behold your mother!"
> —JOHN 19:26, 27

⋧ When Jesus was an infant, Joseph and Mary brought him to the temple according to the custom of their time and dedicated him to God. On that occasion, a pious man named Simeon served as a priest in the temple. When he took the infant into his arms, he believed that this child was the Redeemer for whom he had prayed. In his ecstasy he prophesied the glory of this holy one but warned Mary, "And a sword will pierce through your own soul also."

Mary remembered his words as she watched the boy grow into manhood. Other children were born of Mary and Joseph, but Jesus was her first born. When Joseph died Jesus assumed the responsibility for the care of the family. He did it by carpentry, a trade he had learned from Joseph.

As the years passed, Mary became concerned lest he miss the high calling to which she knew that he was ordained. At the wedding feast in Cana, she called on him to demonstrate his divine powers by turning water into wine. He did it—to please her, for she was his mother and he loved her. After this incident, he felt impelled to fulfill his mission, for the time was at hand. Mary was glad when he called his disciples to follow him and left home—at last her Son would prove himself. The news of his success and acclaim in the first year of his ministry pleased her. But later came ominous reports. There were people who opposed him. His life was endangered.

Going forth with others of her children, she felt that she must bring him home again for his own safety. When they met, however, she knew that it was too late. The holy light in his eyes told her that she could not dissuade him from his mission.

Thereafter anxious months passed until at last came the day when the terrible news was brought to her by John. Mary would have it no other way, she must be with him! That is why she was at Calvary that day, and verily the sword pierced her heart.

Jesus, the Son of God, who was also the son of Mary, in his dying agony was concerned about his mother's welfare. Looking down from the cross, he saw her supported by the strong arms of the young disciple, John. Who would be more suitable to take care of her than this young man whose spirit was so much akin to his own? Still assuming responsibility for his family, Jesus entrusted his mother to John. The Scriptures tell us that John almost immediately took her to his home. Tradition says that he cared for her as long as she lived.

The question might be asked, "Why did Jesus commend her to the care of John in preference to one of her own children?" The answer lies in the fact that in those trying moments John understood more clearly what was happening than Jesus' own brothers and sisters. Brothers in the spirit may be more deeply akin than brothers by blood. Moreover, John was not married and was fully capable of taking care of her.

Jesus could not have given Mary a more worthy son. Mary could not have found a son who would give her greater love.

The Fourth Word

> And at the ninth hour Jesus cried with a loud voice, "Eloi,
> Eloi, lama sabachthani?" which means, "My God, my God,
> why hast thou forsaken me?"   —MARK 15:34

◆§ The first three statements of the Lord which were
spoken from the cross indicate his concern for the welfare
of others. The last four deal with his own physical and
spiritual agony.

Considerable time must have elapsed between the third
and the fourth words. John took Mary to his home and in
that interval it seems that Peter had enough courage to
venture near the cross. Still smitten with shame because he
had denied knowing Jesus the night before, he remained
away from Calvary as long as his conscience permitted him.
Timidly he came upon the scene and noticed that he was
the only disciple present. He may not have known that
John had been there and left with Mary. Standing with
bowed head, ashamed to raise his eyes to Jesus, he heard
the Lord exlaim the fourth word. Later he told it to Mark
who recorded it in his Gospel.

During the period of the sixth to the ninth hour (which
corresponds to 12:00 to 3:00 p.m.) darkness came over the
earth and many of the people left Calvary bewildered by the
eclipse. Just what thoughts occupied the mind of the Son
of God in those hours of darkness, no one knows. It would
be assuming too much for anyone to attempt an explanation
of the Savior's concerns in those sacred moments.

Jesus was human as we are, and his suffering was just as
real as any that we can experience. He is unique in history,
for in him there is a mysterious unity of the human and

the divine. He was both Son of God and son of man. Before the day of crucifixion he had clearly shown how completely he shared our human nature. When he saw the sorrow of Mary and Martha over the death of their brother, Lazarus, he was so moved with sympathy that he wept also. In the Garden of Gethsemane he had prayed fervently that the bitter cup of death on the cross might be taken away. But never did he so unconditionally identify himself with man as he did in this word, "Why hast thou forsaken me?"

In the midst of intense suffering many people have asked a similar question: "Why does this happen to me? Has God forgotten me?" The mind is confused by suffering and under its impact we reach to God for immediate relief. When relief is not promptly forthcoming we tend to blame God for neglect.

Jesus was no less human than others, and in those hours of agony the physical suffering was so intense that the human Jesus called upon God, as any other sufferer might. We thank God for this fourth word. It brings our Savior very near us and assures us that he knows fully the meaning of suffering.

The Fifth Word

> After this, Jesus, knowing that all was now finished, said (to fulfil the scripture), "I thirst." —JOHN 19:28

◄§ This word is recorded by John who had evidently returned after taking Mary to his home. It was at about three o'clock in the afternoon and the darkness that covered the scene was being dispelled by the light of day.

The fourth word, the cry of agony, seemed to relieve the tortured mind of the Savior and a calmness came over his being. John, who understood the spirit of Jesus better than any of the disciples, sensed this composure also for he wrote, "Jesus, knowing that all was now finished, said (to fulfil the scripture), 'I thirst.'" It was only after his work as the Savior was finished that he became conscious of his own physical needs.

He knew all-consuming thirst. His statement about it is the only expression of physical pain that came from his lips through those grueling hours. After such a long time of exposure on the cross, thirst became extremely agonizing—so intense that it overshadowed all the other pains that wracked his tortured body.

All through his life he had practiced the spirit of compassion for suffering people, many of whom he healed. He taught the disciples to visit the sick and the suffering as well as those in prison, and to give a cup of cold water to the thirsty. He told them that he would regard compassion as a service done unto him.

Now upon the cross he expressed his anguish, saying, "I thirst." He had never refused to hear the cry of any person in need. Would anyone in the crowd be moved by his terrible need at this moment? At first it seemed that he would be disappointed. Some who heard him cry, "Eloi, Eloi, lama sabachthani," misunderstood him. Perhaps they spoke Hebrew or Latin and were not conversant with the Aramaic language that Jesus used. "Behold he is calling Elijah," one of them said. "Wait, let us see whether Elijah will come to take him down."

But the milk of human kindness was still flowing in the heart of one of the hardened soldiers. Ashamed to appear to be kind, he also made a slighting remark, but at the same time he took a sponge and after placing it on a stick, he dipped it into the vessel of vinegar and lifted it to the lips of Jesus. This vessel and sponge were brought to the place of execution by some benevolent women of Jerusalem who did it out of kindness for condemned criminals.

The sympathetic act of this soldier has made his memory immortal. It has set him apart from the others on the hill that day. Do we envy him his opportunity? Then let us remember that we also may give our Lord drink. Did he not say: "Truly, I say to you, as you did it to one of the least of these my brethren, you did it to me."

The Sixth Word

When Jesus had received the vinegar, he said, "It is finished"; and he bowed his head and gave up his spirit.

—JOHN 19:30

◄§ An inventor will burn the midnight oil in tireless effort until at last he sees the success of his labor. Every accomplishment of any merit represents toil and a certain amount of suffering, because materials as well as human beings resist change. Jesus worked with the most resistant material on earth, human life. It was his purpose to direct man to God and to bring God to man.

His passion for the welfare of man was obvious in all his

actions. Anyone who wished to do so could readily see that Jesus' chief concern was the happiness of those whom he came into the world to redeem. Might we not expect that he would therefore receive encouragement on every hand, and that the religious forces especially would give him every cooperation? But man resists any change and it was no different in his life. As soon as he was well received by many people, he was also opposed by those who were in power. Thus his life became hemmed in and finally crushed by the evil men who worked against him.

It was heart-breaking for him to have to accept the fact that men would oppose him, more so because he loved so much. In the garden of Gethsemane he accepted the inevitable when he prayed, "If it be possible, let this cup pass from me; nevertheless, not as I will, but as thou wilt."

After that prayer he went ahead courageously doing the Father's business for which he came into the world. On Calvary he permitted evil to do its worst, and it certainly did. In taking upon himself the consequences of man's sin, he redeemed forever all those who accept his sacrifice through faith.

This word, "It is finished," is a cry of victory. His enemies thought that he was utterly defeated and that the world would soon forget him. How amazed they would be were they living today! They could hear people talking about Jesus as if he were still among them—and almost two thousand years have passed since he uttered that brief statement. It is only one word among many that he spoke, but it may well be regarded as the most important single word that was ever uttered.

Jesus was not referring to his own anquish when he said, "It is finished." It was the completion of his divine mission that inspired this word of triumph. Now he had finished the work that his Father had given him to do, bringing at-one-ment between man and God.

Thus, even to the end of his earthly life Jesus' dominant concern was not with his own comfort, but with the eternal salvation of man. His deep concern for the welfare of others has marked his followers ever since. It sets them apart from those who are motivated by selfish interests, according to the measure of his spirit that they have absorbed.

The Seventh Word

> Then Jesus, crying with a loud voice, said, "Father, into thy hands I commit my spirit!" And having said this he breathed his last. —LUKE 23:46

❧ When a person dies, members of his family and others who had loved him try to recall some of the thoughts and words of the one who is gone. They place special importance upon the very last words that he uttered and, in tender remembrance, repeat them again and again.

A hospital chaplain is with many people in the last moments of life. Thus the writer has observed varied reactions to the approach of death. Some people are apprehensive; others are calm. The reaction will depend a good deal on how the person has lived. Those who have known fellowship with God along the way will approach death with much less apprehension than those who have never known the peace of prayer.

On the cross Jesus brought the best example of the way to die. With confidence he addressed his last words to the eternal Father. It is worth noting that the first and the last statements made from the cross both begin with the word "Father." Any fear or apprehension that might otherwise have been in his heart was banished by his complete confidence in God. Although others forsook him and fled, he was not alone. All through his life he was on intimate terms with the Father and here on Calvary that fellowship strengthened him. For a time, he may have felt himself forsaken, just as anyone does at times when the mind is clouded by physical or spiritual suffering. But the moment passed and that peace which passes all human understanding brought calm to his soul again. Prayer is always appropriate in life but especially so in the last moments. Better than anything else it helps to bring confidence.

In this last word Jesus gives the assurance of eternal life to all who have faith in him. He commended his spirit into the hands of the eternal Father. From heaven above he came to earth to dwell among men and point the way to eternal salvation. His work was done magnificently and with this utterance his life in human form came to a conclusion. He would appear to them again after the resurrection in a transformed body, but for all purposes the salvation of man was fully accomplished with his last utterance on Calvary.

Once before, he told his disciples, "And I, when I am lifted up from the earth, will draw all men to myself." That is exactly what has happened. He died that he might live, not in one place but everywhere. His spirit is now available to all who want it and people anywhere can find him when they pray. His spirit returned whence it came, for he and the Father are one and God is everywhere. The eyes of all his followers turn to the cross and find in it what they need for their souls.

Mary, the Mother of the Lord

Blessed are you among women.   —LUKE 1:42

◆§ Mary, the mother of the Lord, was of the house of David. Other than that nothing is known of her birth and childhood. Jesus was her first-born. Later there were children of the marriage of Joseph and Mary whose names are mentioned in the Gospels. Their modest home was in Nazareth where Joseph plied the trade of a carpenter. No doubt Jesus, the eldest son, worked with him and learned carpentry from him. It is believed that Joseph died shortly after the presentation of the twelve-year-old Jesus in the temple, and thereafter Jesus, since he was the oldest, assumed responsibility for the welfare of the family.

In Jesus' teachings there are references to home life. As a boy he must have watched Mary as she went about her work patching garments, preserving the wine in skins, preparing the dough for bread. Furthermore, she must have taught her children the words of Scripture she knew from memory and seen to it that they attended the synagogue. Jesus later quoted the Scripture often; he knew it so well.

Mary, the mother, often became disturbed about her child of God. She saw the years pass and nothing happen. She cherished in her heart the promises of God and the heavenly manifestations surrounding his birth. She knew he was the

Son of God. Yet he was about thirty years old and had given no definite recognition of his mission. Could that have been the reason she urged him to perform the miracle at Cana when he turned water into wine?

Then came the years of his ministry. She saw him grow in popularity and at the same time grow away from her. No longer could she cope with him or understand him. Some may even have whispered that he was sapping his strength—he could not keep up this pace! That is when in desperation she brought his brothers and sisters to the place where he was and begged him to come home.

But he must do the works of him that sent him, and even Mary could not distract him. She returned home with an apprehensive heart; at last it dawned on her that he realized his great mission. Thereafter Mary no longer tried to influence him.

Simeon had prophesied that a sword would pierce her heart and the day when Mary stood beneath the cross on Calvary she knew the meaning of that prophecy. But even there he was concerned about her welfare and gave her into the care of John.

Mary is blessed among women; she has the affection and adoration of many people because God chose her as the one through whom Jesus would live among men and point the way to salvation.

Mary Magdalene

> Mary Magdalene and Mary the mother of Joses saw where
> he was laid. —MARK 15:47

◦§ There are a number of Marys who were closely associated with the Lord: Mary, his mother; Mary, the wife of
Cleophas; Mary, the mother of Mark; Mary, the sister of
Lazarus and Martha, and Mary Magdalene. The latter Mary
is identified by the place where she was born and reared,
Magdala in Galilee. Just how she happened to meet Jesus
is not known, but Luke gives a clue in the second verse of
the eighth chapter where he designates her as one whom the
Lord healed of a mental disturbance.

It is altogether possible that she was brought to him by
some of her loved ones and the Master healed her. After that
she became a faithful follower and was among those few
who witnessed the crucifixion.

Through the ages Mary has been identified with the "great
sinner" in the seventh chapter of Luke who anointed the
head and feet of Jesus with costly ointment. For that reason
the name "Magdalene" has come to mean a "fallen" woman.
There are many paintings that depict her as a penitent sinner.
During the Middle Ages she was portrayed in the mystery
plays as being in league with Satan until the Lord freed her
of this bondage. It is to be deplored that an honorable person
should be so misrepresented. There is no basis in Scripture
for designating Mary Magdalene that way and it is time that
her name be cleared of such associations.

Every reference to her in the Scripture indicates her faithfulness and purity. Most likely she was at one time mentally
ill; after she was healed she decided in deep gratitude to

devote her life to the service of the One who did so much to help her and others. No doubt she shared her resources with the apostles. They were not gainfully employed during their discipleship and assistance had to come from those who were in a position to share their possessions.

Of her devotion there can be no doubt. She faced the shame and ridicule of Calvary when her Lord was crucified. Then that first Good Friday evening she was with those few loyal ones who removed his body from the cross, wrapped it in linen according to the custom of the time, and placed it in the new tomb donated by Joseph of Arimathea.

On Easter morning she was among those who went to the tomb with sweet spices intending to anoint the body. There she was a recipient of the good news that he was risen and alive.

Mary of Magdala is remembered in much legend that was widely spread in the Early Church. Some of these traditions are contradictory. One story says that she went into what is now France and retired to a life of contemplation. Another says that after the death of Mary, the mother of Jesus, she accompanied John to Ephesus where she spent the rest of her life in Christian service.

More Than They Expected

Why do you seek the living among the dead? —LUKE 24:5

◦§ It was a very sad Friday for those who loved Jesus. Among them was Joseph of Arimathea, a member of the

Sanhedrin or Council that condemned Jesus. But he had not favored the action. The Scripture relates specifically that Joseph of Arimathea did not consent to the sentence imposed on Jesus. What was one dissenting voice against the mob!

Much disturbed by the crucifixion, Joseph went personally to the Roman governor, Pontius Pilate, of whom he asked permission to claim the body of Jesus. Then, before the setting of the sun that ushered in the Sabbath day, he with a small group of the faithful women went out to Calvary where they tenderly removed his body from the cross, wrapped it in linen, and carried it to a new tomb. Joseph donated this burial place for the one whom he respected and loved. After placing the body within, they reverently withdrew and the opening of the tomb was closed with a large stone. By that time darkness was coming on, and they returned to their homes.

There was no time for the women to prepare the body with spices for the burial as was customary. Since the next day was the Sabbath, they had to wait until the following day to perform this service of love. So, it was early on Sunday morning that they went again to the garden, taking their spices with them with the intention of preparing the body. Sadly they walked along in the dim light of the dawning day, wondering if they could roll away the heavy stone.

Reaching the burial place, they found the stone already rolled away. Their first thought was that someone had opened the grave and carried away the body of Jesus. Could it have been enemies of his? Could Joseph have changed his mind? Had not enough indignities already been inflicted upon his sacred person! In their perplexity they looked to one another for an explanation, when all at once two angels appeared as men in shining garments.

The appearance of the heavenly visitors filled them with still more fear momentarily. As they humbly bowed one of the angels asked, "Why do you seek the living among the dead? Remember how he told you, while he was still in Galilee, that the Son of man must be delivered into the hands of sinful men, and be crucified, and on the third day rise."

It was news almost too good to be true. They had started on a mission of love, to prepare the body of their Lord for burial, and now the angel announced that he was not dead at all! It is extremely difficult to believe something as wonderful as that on the spur of the moment. But they accepted the glad word and all but Mary Magdalene left the garden to tell the good news to the other disciples. The one who they thought was lost to them forever was given back and soon their tears of sorrow would be changed to expressions of joy. That first Easter morning God rewarded their devotion far beyond anything that they expected.

What If He Had Not Risen!

If Christ has not been raised, then our preaching is in vain and your faith is in vain. . . . For if the dead are not raised, then Christ has not been raised. If Christ has not been raised, your faith is futile and you are still in your sins. Then those also who have fallen asleep in Christ have perished. —I CORINTHIANS 15:14, 16-18

"I don't believe it! It never happened before! I don't see why it happened to him!" A few people in Corinth were making remarks to that effect and evidently someone either wrote Paul about it or told him. No one could question the resurrection of Jesus without disturbing Paul terribly. He was never more eloquent than in this chapter. Here his thoughts flow so quickly that his secretary must have had difficulty in taking his dictation.

There is a story about a medieval warrior who conquered a city, imprisoning its leaders, and announcing his intention to burn it to the ground. The imprisoned officials were prevented from communicating with anyone on the outside and there awaited what they thought would be certain death. Their king, they believed, had been killed in the battle; but it so happened that he managed to escape and was raising forces at that very moment with the purpose of taking his city again. Unexpectedly, he returned with an army and routed the enemy. The despondent prisoners could hardly believe their ears when they heard people shouting, "Long live the king! Long live the king!" The one who they thought was dead, was very much alive and had returned to liberate them from the grave. One can hardly imagine their joy. What if someone had come to them in the midst of their rejoicing and said, "I am sorry to have to tell you that a mistake has been made. This man was not your king after all. You are still doomed!"

Paul wrote the Corinthians that a denial of the resurrection of Jesus had very serious implications. "If Christ has not been raised, your faith is futile and you are still in your sins." If Christ had not risen Paul would have to retrace his steps and tell all the people, "I made a mistake; I am very sorry. You can go back to your old lifeless beliefs, there is no eternal life for you."

So far as forgiveness of sins is concerned, if Christ be not risen he was just one more martyr in a long line of heroes who gave their lives for their convictions. He would have no more power to forgive sins than Stephen or any other person who died rather than deny his ideals.

"Then those also who have fallen asleep in Christ have perished." The host of Christians who devoted their lives to the service of the Lord would not live again. They would be hopelessly gone forever. Such thoughts are terribly disturbing to us today, but no more so than they were to Paul and those early Christians. He lost no time in writing to the congregation in Corinth so that they would not let anyone destroy their faith in one of the most important divine acts of the Son of God. The resurrection was not a proof of his divinity, it was the natural result of it. To deny it meant a repudiation of one of the most meaningful events of his marvelous life.

For Us

The next day he saw Jesus coming toward him, and said, "Behold, the Lamb of God, who takes away the sin of the world!"   —JOHN 1:29

◄§ The land of Tibet became prominent in international news flashes when the Chinese communists invaded it and its rulers fled to India only to return after a few months. This almost inaccessible plateau country, south of China and North of India in the Himalaya mountains, was ruled by a religious cult. Few white men ever explored the land and lived to tell about it, but some have succeeded in that hazardous task.

One who did return tells about a religious ceremony that he witnessed. He was permitted to see it only after he was accepted into the cult and lived among the people for a number of years. He knew the initiate, a rather young man, who desired to go into seclusion in order to find God and experience forgiveness. The candidate vowed never to speak to a human being again and to live his life apart from the world. Priests and others followed him to a cave into which he entered. Then the priests proceeded to seal the opening with stones, one after another, until it was completely closed except for one removable stone.

Thereafter, each day a priest came to the cave with a dish of food. He pulled out the loose stone and removed the empty dish and pushed in the other. This was the only attention the man received from the outside world. In the cave he lived his life in darkness. Day and night came and went and he lost track of time. His body became pale and emaciated but he did not know it; his voice became a cracking mumble as he said his prayers. Summer and winter came and went, but after a while the change in temperature inside the cave was so slight that he could not tell the difference and he was no longer interested.

Then one day the priest found the dish of food untouched. He removed it and pushed in another. After six days, the priests came and sealed the one movable stone permanently into the wall of the entrance. The young man had been relieved of his living death.

He never heard about Jesus and the sacrifice on Calvary. No doubt God recognized his devotion, but the Almighty does not desire the sacrifice of human life. He can be found while we live a normal life, for he speaks to us in many ways. Through faith in Jesus Christ we are saved. His blood was shed on Calvary so that we might have forgiveness, abundant life, and salvation. We appropriate his sacrifice and it becomes sufficient for us when we accept him as our personal Savior. That message of God's plan of salvation was unknown to the young man in Tibet. It has been revealed to us through his Word, and when we sincerely dedicate ourselves to him we will know that it was for us that the Lord did it.

Peter

> And he said to them, "But who do you say that I am?" And Peter answered, "The Christ of God."   —LUKE 9:20

When we think about the disciples of Jesus the one who usually comes to mind first of all is Peter. His original name, Simeon or Simon, was a common one of that day. He must also have had an Aramaic name, Kepha or Cephas, which means "rock." The Greek equivalent for it is "Peter." In the biblical account Jesus actually called him Peter or "Rock" only three times; otherwise he generally used his common name, Simon.

Peter and his younger brother, Andrew, made their living at fishing. They probably owned their own boat as well as their modest homes, and sold their fish in the market. Peter was married; on one occasion the Lord healed his mother-in-law who was ill with a fever.

This disciple of the Lord spoke with a Galilean accent. He appears to have been a courageous, sincere man. He gained preeminence among the apostles because of his ability to make a decision quickly. A person who makes decisions quickly runs the risk of making mistakes, but in any situation someone must decide the issue and assume the responsibility. He is the one who is also blamed when things go wrong.

Being of a highly emotional nature he could become very enthusiastic, but when disappointment came he was dejected to the lowest depths. He is loved so much even today because he was very human, though in his better moments he rose to godly heights.

After the apostles had been with Jesus for some time he wanted an expression of their faith in him. They were on their way to Caesarea Philipi, which was built on a bluff. The Jordan river has its source beneath that rock. As they were walking along, Jesus asked them to tell him who people said that he was. After they reported various opinions Jesus pointedly asked the question, "But who do you say that I am?" It was the impulsive Peter who was spokesman for the group: "The Christ of God." According to Matthew Jesus said to him, "And I tell you, you are Peter, and on this rock I will build my church, and the powers of death shall not prevail against it." This was the Lord's assurance that his church would be built upon the rock of such faith as Peter had professed.

Through his constant association with the Lord, and as he grew in experience, Peter's temperament became more stable. His sincerity and consecration gave him a place of leadership in the Church, in whose interest he became an indefatigable worker. Like Paul he made missionary journeys, and he went as far as Rome. Early writers tell about his residence at Rome and record that he and Paul founded the congregation there.

Mark must have visited him in Rome. He wrote his Gospel after Peter's death on the basis of the many things Peter had told him about Jesus. According to tradition Peter was crucified during a persecution in Nero's reign. When he was sentenced to the cross he chose to die head downward because he felt that he was not worthy to die in the same manner as his Lord.

James

> And going on from there he saw two other brothers, James the son of Zebedee and John his brother, in the boat with Zebedee their father, mending their nets, and he called them. —MATTHEW 4:21

◄§ James and John were sons of Zebedee who made their living as fishermen on the sea of Galilee. They were successful in their business to the extent that they had hired servants. Their mother, Salome, was undoubtedly one of those companions of Jesus who cared for the daily needs of his life. In later years these women became known as the deaconesses of the Church. James probably first learned to know Jesus through his mother. At any rate he was prepared to follow when the Master called the two brothers from the boat where they were mending nets.

Having made the decision, James never wavered. He became one of the three disciples in whom the Lord placed utmost confidence. He came to that position of trust even though, like his brother, he had a hot, quick temper. The two sons must have been influenced greatly by their mother. On one occasion she impetuously asked Jesus to give the two best places in his kingdom to her sons. Jesus told her that places in his kingdom would go to those who deserved them, and if her sons proved worthy they would certainly be honored.

Jesus noticed their tempers and called them "Sons of Thunder." Once when he and his disciples were refused hospitality in a Samaritan village, James wanted him to call down fire from heaven and destroy the whole town. Jesus taught him an important lesson in self-discipline when he ignored the insult and went on to another town where they were welcome. As he continued to associate with Jesus, he learned to control his temper and to direct it into useful and constructive channels. Jesus had a high regard for James. He is often mentioned among the three apostles who shared some of the most sacred moments in Jesus' life. The others were Peter and John.

James became the first of the twelve apostles to give his life for the faith. The Acts relates that he was killed by the sword on the orders of Herod Agrippa. According to an ancient writer, Clement of Alexandria, Herod would have seized Peter also, but his time had not yet come.

This same authority wrote about the death of James, saying that the man who brought him to the judgment seat was so impressed with his testimony and the demeanor of his life that he also confessed faith in Jesus. Both were condemned and led away for execution. On the way this man asked James to forgive him for the treatment he had accorded him.

49

James said, "Peace be to thee," and kissed him. This gesture of forgiveness was his last act before he was beheaded. James, the son of Salome, proved himself worthy of one of the important places in Jesus' kingdom.

John

> And when he came to the house, he permitted no one to enter with him, except Peter and John and James, and the father and mother of the child. —LUKE 8:51

◆§ Jairus was a ruler of the synagogue. His only daughter, a child of twelve, lay dying. In his extremity he hurried to Jesus and begged him to come to the house. But the crowd made it difficult for Jesus to move, and soon a messenger arrived from the ruler's house to tell them it was too late: "Your daughter is dead; do not trouble the Teacher any more." Jesus heard it and reassured the father. "Do not fear," he said, "only believe, and she shall be well." They made their way to Jairus' home. When they came to the room where the child was, Jesus permitted only Peter, James, and John to go in with the parents.

With Peter and James, John formed the inner circle of the apostles. He is believed to have been the youngest of the Twelve. Of all the apostles he probably understood best the mind and spirit of the Master.

John, like his brother James, was a "son of thunder." He too needed to learn to control his temper and to direct it into useful and constructive channels.

John's devotion to Jesus was so sincere that he became known as the disciple who loved the Lord. Jesus returned his affection. The incident that most clearly shows Jesus' regard for him occurred on Calvary. Concerned about his mother, Jesus knew that he could entrust her to no one better or more sympathetic than John. Although Mary had other children, Jesus was the oldest and accepted responsibility for her welfare. From the cross he commended her to the care of John. Tradition says that the apostle took her into his home that same day and cared for her until she died. Read the Calvary scene in the Gospel of John carefully and you will note that certain statements made by Jesus during the crucifixion are omitted. This could indicate that Jesus spoke them while John was away, taking Mary to his home.

After her death John became a missionary. His travels led him into Asia Minor, where he made the church in Ephesus his spiritual home. During an outbreak of persecution under the Roman Emperor Domitian he was sentenced to slave labor in the salt mines on the Isle of Patmos. It is believed by biblical scholars that he wrote the book of Revelation while he was a prisoner there. The book was probably written in sections and taken secretly to the congregations on the mainland.

John was an old man when he was pardoned. He went back to Ephesus to live out his years. He was a highly respected and beloved member of the congregation. Love was the great theme of his teaching. He died at a ripe old age, toward the close of the first century, and was laid tenderly to rest by those who loved and respected him for the great soldier of the cross that he was.

Andrew

. . . and Andrew his brother.   —MATTHEW 10:2

◄§ Peter is usually considered to be the firt apostle called by Jesus, but the records indicate that it was his brother, Andrew, who first knew Jesus. Andrew was a disciple of John the Baptist and was with him when Jesus came to John as he was preaching on the banks of the Jordan river. The Baptist directed his disciples to the Lord when he said, "Behold the Lamb of God who takes away the sin of the world!" Thereafter Andrew became a follower of Jesus.

Andrew and Peter were brothers by blood, and they were brothers in spirit also. Before long the words and the personality of the great Teacher meant so much to Andrew that he had to bring Peter to him. This one act is enough to merit the lasting gratitude of all followers of the Lord, because he thus introduced to Jesus the one who was destined to become the dominant leader of the early Church.

Little is written about Andrew in the Scriptures. He must have been a true disciple of the lowly and humble Nazarene, because as time went on Peter came to the foreground more and more and Andrew receded into anonymity. Humility is surely a virtue when it moves a man to relinquish a position of leadership to another who is better qualified for the part. Andrew had only good will for his able brother. He wanted more than anything else to see the teachings of his Lord and Savior prosper.

Early Christian writers continue with the story of the followers of Jesus where the book of the Acts leaves off. These writers indicate that Andrew became a great preacher of the gospel. He made missionary journeys into Greece and then northward into Scythia, which later became a part of Russia. For that reason he became the special patron saint of the Russian Orthodox Church.

This humble, self-effacing apostle devoted his life entirely to the Lord, even to the extent of martyrdom. According to tradition, he was crucified on November 30, in what is now a portion of Greece. Because he would not compromise his convictions and offer incense to the gods, the proconsul ordered him to die upon a cross. The cross used was in the form of an X, and ever since it has been known as St. Andrew's cross. In this form the cross is seen on the steeples of many Greek churches.

Bartholomew or Nathanael

> Nathanael said to him, "Can anything good come out of Nazareth?" Philip said to him, "Come and see."
> —JOHN 1:46

⮞ Bartholomew is one of the twelve apostles whom it is difficult to identify. He is mentioned in the list of the apostles given by Matthew, Mark, and Luke. John omits his name; instead he places Nathanael right after Philip, the position in which Bartholomew is listed by the other Gospel writers.

These facts lead many biblical scholars to the conclusion that Bartholomew and Nathanael are the same person with two names. It was common practice in those days to apply two or more names to a person. Matthew is called Levi too.

Peter is known also as Cephas and Simon. So it is altogether probable that Bartholomew and Nathanael are the same person.

John tells about the calling of Nathanael. He probably was the brother of Philip who learned to know the Lord first and then invited Nathanael to meet him. When Nathanael was told that Jesus came from Nazareth he did not share Philip's enthusiasm. Evidently his opinion of Nazareth was not very good; he asked, "Can any good thing come out of Nazareth?" Bartholomew Nathanael expected big things to come only from big cities.

Nevertheless, he went with his brother. When he met Jesus, the Lord complimented him as a man in whom there was no guile. This observation rather startled him and he asked, "How do you know me?" Thereupon Jesus told him that before Philip called him, when he was beneath a fig tree, he saw him there. This man without guile was so impressed that he was willing then and there to become a follower.

The Scriptures are silent about his life as one of the Twelve. In this instance again the early church writers supply traditions about his activities. According to Eusebius and Jerome, Nathanael preached the gospel in lands eastward as far as India. Eusebius lived in the third century and could very well have received his information from those who passed it down a few generations by word of mouth.

Other Asiatic countries also have been named as places where Nathanael preached and worked, especially Armenia where he is said to have been crucified, head down. There is little doubt that this man devoted his life to the spreading of the gospel. Since other apostles went in other directions he may have chosen to go eastward, desiring to make the kingdom of his Master world-wide.

Matthew

> As Jesus passed on from there, he saw a man called Matthew
> sitting at the tax office; and he said to him, "Follow me."
> And he rose and followed him.   —MATTHEW 9:9

✑ The office of a tax collector is important, but hardly popular in any age. While the tax collector today gathers only
what he is instructed by law to gather, his position is not
admired. In Jesus' day a tax collector (or publican) in the
Jewish provinces was considered a social outcast.

They probably had good reasons for treating the ordinary
publican with disdain. Many publicans were dishonest and
extracted more than they had a right to collect. The Jews did
not like the Roman overlordship in the first place, and they
felt that anyone who collected taxes for the Romans was
betraying his own people. They classified such a person so-
cially with harlots.

Matthew was a publican. He may have decided that he
wanted to be a rich man more than anything else and saw in
that position a means of realizing his hopes. Most likely he
lived in the Roman section of the city because Jewish neighbors would not want him around.

The name Matthew means "gift of God." Whether this
name was given to him by his parents or by Jesus after he
became one of the Twelve is not known. He is also called
Levi by Mark and Luke. He was reared in a pious Jewish
home where he was taught that the Messiah would some day
come and liberate his people. Matthew must have known
that his parents would never approve his collecting of taxes
for the government from which they prayed to be delivered.
No doubt his conscience often bothered him on that score.

In his position as a public officer he heard a lot of news and his attention would surely be drawn to Jesus. He may have heard him speak on some occasions and the words of the great Teacher seemed to him to apply directly to his needs; they awakened his conscience, which spoke to him in an ever more demanding voice. Then one day it happened! Jesus came near his place of business and Matthew watched him intently. He saw Jesus coming directly to him; Jesus paused a moment, looked at Matthew with understanding in his kind face, and said, "Follow me."

That was all Matthew needed! This invitation was encouragement enough to give him fortitude to obey the dictates of his conscience. Then and there he relinquished his position and became a devoted follower of Jesus.

Matthew never regretted that decision. He found in Jesus peace of heart and mind. Out of his intimate association with the Son of God he wrote the Gospel of Matthew to prove to his own people that Jesus was the promised Messiah for whom they had devoutly prayed.

Tradition says that Matthew became a Christian missionary who brought the gospel to Africa, where he settled in what is now Abyssinia. The Coptic Christians of that country are believed to be his spiritual descendants.

Thomas

> Then he said to Thomas, "Put your finger here, and see my hands; and put out your hand, and place it in my side; do not be faithless, but believing." Thomas answered him, "My Lord and my God!" —JOHN 20:27, 28

Thomas was also called Didymus, which means "twin." This name may have been given him by his parents after his twin brother or sister died.

When Jesus called the apostles he chose men with various natures and personalities. Thomas was the very opposite of the impetuous and trusting Peter. His attitude was pessimistic; he did not want to accept anything until it had been proved to him.

Thomas loved and admired Jesus, but he was quite sure nothing would ever come of his ministry. At one time when Jesus intended to go to Jerusalem, it was Thomas who said, "Let us also go, that we may die with him." He knew Jesus had many enemies who would eventually kill him and he thought that would be the end of it all. Despite this gloomy attitude, he had the courage to volunteer to go along to the bitter end. It is much easier to follow a leader when there is confidence in the success of his cause.

After the crucifixion Thomas could see no reason why the apostles should continue together. To his way of thinking it was all over, and with a heavy heart he decided to readjust his life to another way of living. That is why he was not present with the others when the resurrected Lord appeared to them that first Easter Sunday night. Thus Thomas missed a wonderful experience because his skepticism kept him away. The other apostles lost no time in telling him about the living Lord. Half believing, half doubting, he resumed meeting with them.

It was a week later when the Lord appeared again and on that occasion Thomas was present. It must have been a shock to this doubting man. At first he did not want to believe what he saw with his own eyes. When the Lord noticed his hesitancy, he invited him to touch his wounds with his fingers. This was enough proof for Thomas. We are not told that he actually touched him, but he did at last confess complete faith when he said, "My Lord and my God."

Thereafter the Scriptures remain silent about Thomas. According to tradition, he traveled eastward as far as India preaching the gospel of Jesus. There he is supposed to have died a martyr's death.

Philip

The next day Jesus decided to go to Galilee. And he found Philip and said to him, "Follow me." —JOHN 1:43

◄§ Philip was from Bethsaida, the city of Andrew and Peter. Little is known about his life before he became a follower of Jesus. His name is mentioned with the twelve apostles in the list given by each Gospel writer, but only John records incidents in the ministry of Jesus in which Philip figured prominently.

After he became acquainted with Jesus he was so well impressed that he found Nathanael, a friend or brother, and invited him to meet Jesus also. In the invitation he expressed his conviction that Jesus of Nazareth was the one of whom Moses and the prophets had written.

People with convictions usually become good evangelists. More followers have been won to the cause of Christ by personal invitation than in any other way. Philip found in Jesus something he needed and prized, and he wanted to share it with Nathanael.

It is some time before Philip appears again in the Gospel narrative. Jesus had finished talking to a throng of about five thousand people. They stayed longer than he expected and they were getting hungry. In this dilemma he turned to Philip and asked, "How are we to buy bread, so that these people can eat?" The Scriptures say he asked the questions to test Philip. He must have known Philip quite well, for this cautious disciple answered the way he anticipated: "Two hundred denarii would not buy enough bread for each of them to get a little."

Philip was so much concerned about the cost that he did not hear the question. Purposely Jesus had not asked how much it would cost to feed them—he asked where the food could be secured. Philip must have been the watchdog of the treasury and all he thought about was the cost.

The Christian Church needs men like Philip today. We have need of cautious people who keep the enthusiastic ones from going too far into debt for kingdom purposes. But it is a blessing that not all church officials are as cautious as Philip; if they were the Church would never venture. It also needs men and women who have faith enough to go ahead even when there is not enough cash available to do the job. The courageous ones are seldom permitted to go too far because there are always enough Philips to keep progress in moderation with the question, "And tell us, where do you think the money is coming from for such a program?"

In this instance Jesus taught Philip, and all other Philips, an important truth. He used a few fish and a few loaves of bread and fed five thousand people. Those who would be too cautious in the Lord's work must not overlook the fact that it is the *Lord's* work and that a venturesome program will succeed if it is in accordance with his holy will.

James the Less

... James the son of Alphaeus. —MATTHEW 10:3

◄§ Three men by the name of James are mentioned in the New Testament as being closely associated with Jesus. The first is James, the brother of John, one of the two sons of Zebedee. The second is James, the brother of the Lord; and the third is James, the son of Alphaeus. The other two so far outshone James Alphaeus that he is called James the Less.

His name is mentioned with the other disciples by each of the evangelists, but beyond that nothing is said about him. A tremendous amount of biblical research has gone into the attempt to find out who he was and why Jesus included him among the Twelve. Various theories have been developed. One is that James' mother was named Mary and belonged to the followers of Jesus. Through her he became acquainted with the Lord, as Mark did through his mother. Another theory is that he was a brother of Simon Zelotes, another of the apostles. Some scholars believe that his father and Joseph were brothers and that for this reason he was considered by the Master a member of the family, the only one who confessed faith in him before his ascension.

No one can prove any of these theories, but there is no denying the fact that he was one of the Twelve. The Lord had reasons, known only to him, why he chose James Alphaeus for this high honor. The very fact that he was among the first to follow Jesus is an indication that he was a man of deep sincerity and good judgment.

Although James Alphaeus is not mentioned as making any outstanding contributions to the work of Jesus, we have no reason to think that it was a mistake to invite him to be one of the Twelve. He is typical of the millions of sincere followers of the Lord through the ages who have been content to do their share unnoticed and without applause.

There are some people in any church or organization who have marked ability and who make significant contributions as leaders, but at the same time they let it be known that they are important. The praise of others spurs them on to even more intensive work, sometimes to the point of self-sacrifice. What they would do without expressions of appreciation can only be conjectured.

In any church or organization there are also many sincere people who wish to remain unknown. They may not possess unusual ability or have much material wealth to share, but the heart is there none the less and they do what they can without applause. In many instances their smaller contribution involves a greater personal sacrifice than what is done in a big way out of more abundant resources or talents.

The only legend about James Alphaeus is to the effect that after the Lord's ascension he became a missionary in southern Palestine and also in Egypt, where he was crucified.

Simon the Cananaean

. . . Simon the Cananaean.   —MATTHEW 10:4

❦ The name of this Simon is included in each list of the apostles given by the evangelists. Otherwise there is no reference to him in the New Testament. There is no doubt, however, that he was one of those chosen by the Lord to compose the intimate circle of his followers. Jesus had disciples other than the Twelve. Though we cannot tell their number, the Scriptures refer to the Seventy. It may be that from these Jesus chose some of the twelve apostles who were to be his almost constant companions and upon whom he relied to transmit his gospel to future generations. That he chose wisely is obvious, for his teachings became well known despite the fact that he did not record any of them in writing. Only the Word of God could have been so thoroughly preserved. Simon the Cananaean was one of those through whom the Lord chose to transmit the words of eternal life.

Simon was a man of ardor. He is called Zelotes or Zealot by Luke, who knew him well. He may have been called a zealot for various reasons, the most important being his ardent nature. Like Peter, he was enthusiastic about the cause of Christ. No doubt the personal sacrifices that he made in order to be one of the Twelve and his willingness to perform any service for the Lord, helped to give him the name, Zealot.

The members of a revolutionary Galilean party were called Zealots also. They were people who were impatient with the Roman occupation and with the local officials who permitted the Romans to rule them. It is believed by some authorities that John the Baptist belonged to this group, but there is nothing in the Scriptures or later writings to substantiate that view. It was a minority group. If Simon belonged to it, he is to be admired for having the courage of his convictions. Perhaps that is why the Lord chose to use him in his service.

Sometimes the Church may make a mistake by excluding from its fellowship smaller groups who are not in full accord with its position on certain issues. The ardor of these people might serve the Church well if their interest could be gained. We are frequently told that church people lack zeal and warmth. Where this is true, one reason may be that persons or groups who have a fiery ardor for their convictions have been excluded from membership.

There are various traditions about Simon the Cananaean: that he did missionary work in Egypt and in Britain; that he labored in Persia and Babylonia. He is one of those among the twelve apostles about whom we wish we could know a good deal more than the records reveal.

Judas Lebbaeus Thaddaeus

. . . and Thaddaeus. —MATTHEW 10:3

Identifying this apostle poses knotty problems. He is not clearly delineated in the New Testament records. In the lists of the apostles we find three names that in all likelihood indicate this one person. The names are Judas, Lebbaeus, and Thaddaeus. The fact that Judas is mentioned in two of the Gospel listings and Lebbaeus Thaddaeus in the other two has led scholars to think all these names refer to the same apostle.

He is not to be confused with Judas Iscariot. The name Judas was very popular in those days. It may be that this apostle bore the name until Judas Iscariot brought disgrace upon it, and thereafter preferred to be known as Lebbaeus so that no one would connect him with the betrayal of Jesus.

The only reference to Judas' career occurs in John 14:22, and here the writer is careful to note which Judas he means: "Judas (not Iscariot) said to him, 'Lord, how is it that you will manifest yourself to us, and not to the world?'" Jesus had been trying to assure the disciples that they had no cause to be troubled about his forthcoming death; he would not leave them desolate, but would come to them. Judas wanted the whole world, and not the disciples only, to see the fulfillment of his Master's promise.

About the life of this apostle in the early history of the Church we know nothing for certain. We have many legends about his missionary activity, and these give us reason to believe that Judas was faithful all his days. Like the other apostles, he did not waver from the faith that in Jesus he had found "the way, and the truth, and the life."

Judas Iscariot

> . . . and Judas Iscariot, who betrayed him.
>
> —MATTHEW 10:4

◄§ Judas was a man of Kerioth, a town in northern Judea, whom Jesus called to be one of the Twelve. Here is a man who might have been great, but today the fact most clearly remembered in connection with his life is that he betrayed the Lord. Whatever good Judas did is all overshadowed by this one act of disloyalty.

Sometimes an otherwise good and wholesome life is wrecked by one big mistake that reveals an inherent weakness of character. This truth, however, does not apply in its entirety to Judas. Some of the Gospel writers indicate that he showed signs of moral weakness before the act of betrayal. John relates that he was a thief and that he was predisposed to evil for quite some time before Satan put it into his mind to betray the Lord. Thus, according to John, Judas did not live a wholesome life spoiled by one big sin, but rather a life of little sins that grew into a terrible mistake.

Both Matthew and Luke seem to think that it was Judas' love of money that caused him to perform this despicable service for the enemies of Jesus. Thirty pieces of silver, although not a large amount of money, were enough to tempt him beyond his power to resist. That observation seems true to his character; if he stole money from the apostles' common treasury from which there could not have been much to steal, the offer of thirty pieces of silver would have tempted him greatly.

Why Jesus chose him to be one of the Twelve is a problem not easily understood. The Lord seems to have known for some time prior to the act that Judas would betray him. Luke explains it by saying, "Satan entered into Judas." To believe that he was deliberately chosen for this purpose by the Lord and became a traitor against his will is not in harmony with our understanding of the mind and heart of the Master. What Judas did was done voluntarily.

Smitten with guilt, he tried to return the money he had received for the betrayal, but the authorities would not take it because it was blood money. In the end they used it to buy a field in which to bury paupers. Judas hanged himself. Thus a man who had a most wonderful opportunity failed utterly. He brought lasting disgrace upon a name that was once popular and loved.

Matthias

And they cast lots for them, and the lot fell on Matthias; and he was enrolled with the eleven apostles.

—ACTS 1:26

◄§ With the death of Judas Iscariot the circle of the Twelve was broken. From the time of the crucifixion until the Lord's ascension he appeared to the eleven apostles, the Seventy, and others on a number of occasions. The apostles were convinced that they had a mission to fulfill in the world. Jesus promised them the gift of the Holy Spirit to guide them in that mission.

The Eleven continued to meet with other believers, and devoted themselves to prayer and spiritual preparation for the reception of his Spirit. During this period they decided to choose another to fill the vacant place in their group. They felt that the new member must be a person who knew the Lord, who had come under the influence of his teaching often, and who was a witness to the resurrection.

Jesus had disciples other than the twelve apostles during

his ministry. There was that larger company usually referred to as the Seventy, who also were faithful but who were not called to leave their homes and employment for constant companionship with him. Then when the time came to choose the twelfth apostle the believers were convinced that he should come from this larger circle of the faithful.

Two men were nominated, Matthias, and Joseph called Barsabus whose surname was Justus. Both were of excellent character, devoted to the cause of the Lord. At a meeting of the faithful, evidently called for that purpose, the Followers of the Way, as they were soon to be known, prayed for guidance in the choice and had an election. When the lots were counted Matthias was the chosen one. Thereby he became the twelfth apostle.

In this instance democratic principles were used to choose a spiritual leader, and that was in a day when democracy was not generally practiced. The influence of the teachings of Jesus is seen in this first official act of his followers, and this principle of the Lord was destined to grow in importance and practice until it finally bore fruit in the history of the democratic nations of the world. It is a principle of Christianity that is opposed today by autocratic or totalitarian thinking.

Nothing more is known historically about the work of Matthias. He may have tried to write a life of Jesus, because in the third and fourth centuries a Gospel by Matthias was in circulation among the Christians. This writing, however, was never accepted as authentic or as inspired by the Holy Spirit, and it was not included among the writings of our New Testament.

The Good Samaritan

> Which of these three, do you think, proved neighbor to the man who fell among the robbers? —LUKE 10:36

⋙ No one knows the name of the Good Samaritan. Jesus purposely refrained from identifying him. That good man would not have wanted anyone to thank him.

A minister was driving his car on the highway at dusk when two cars came together in a head-on collision about a block ahead of him. Both cars were thrown off the highway but remained on their wheels. Hurriedly pulling over to the side of the road, the minister got out of his car to help the victims. Soon another motorist also stopped to help.

In one of the two cars was the driver, a woman, slumped unconscious in the front seat. There were three people in the second car: a woman driver, another who was evidently her mother, and a boy about seven years old. The driver was stunned, the older lady was hysterical, and the boy's face was covered with blood from a wound on his forehead.

The two men removed the unconscious woman carefully from the car and placed her on a blanket. Then the clergyman helped the older woman and the child into his car and drove to the next town, a mile farther on that road. He took them directly to a doctor's office. The nurse took charge while he called the police and told them to send an ambulance and to proceed to the scene of the accident.

Fortunately, the boy's wound was superficial and the grandmother soon regained her composure. The minister volunteered to return them to the injured mother. As they approached the scene of the accident they saw the glow of fire which indicated that one of the cars was burning. He managed to get through the congestion of traffic with the aid of a state trooper. Two ambulances were there waiting for his passengers. The boy was permitted to go with his mother and grandmother to a hospital in the city through which they had just passed.

The minister never again saw the man who helped him remove the two women from the cars. In the excitement no one thought of asking the identity of the two men who helped the victims. The clergyman arrived an hour late for his appointment in the town and excused himself by saying that he had been unavoidably detained.

The next day, the morning press of the nearby city printed the details of the accident, relating that the two women were recovering in a local hospital because "an unidentified Good Samaritan" had helped them. By removing the women from the cars, the reporter said, the life of one of them had been saved.

No one ever learned who the two men were. Evidently neither of them wanted to be thanked for what he did. Like the Good Samaritan, they found wounded people by the side of the road and helped them with no thought of reward.

The Identifying Badge

By this all men will know that you are my disciples, if you have love for one another. —JOHN 13:35

When members of an organization come to its annual convention they are asked to register so that there will be a record of their attendance. Usually each one is given a badge with the name and address of the wearer clearly printed on it. This identification serves a number of purposes. It helps another who cannot remember the name. It may serve as a meal ticket. Most of all it proclaims to anyone who is interested that the wearer is a member of the organization. Thus he is set apart from others and he is a marked man as long as he wears the badge.

Jesus recommended an identifying badge for his disciples, one that would set them apart so that they could readily be distinguished by anyone. This mark was not celluloid or ribbon; it was a way of life.

In those days a Christian's attitude was quite different from that of his neighbors and friends. Popular belief was that might was right, and that love, compassion, and sympathy were weaknesses of character. Those officials who showed mercy and consideration did not long remain in office. Hate your enemies and love your friends—such was the current philosophy of human relations.

Jesus' followers believed in a different way of living. He taught them to love their enemies and to pray for those who persecuted them. He urged them to love one another. To the extent that those who professed faith in him took his teaching seriously they must have stood out sharply in their pagan environment. One of the historians of that period was moved to exclaim, "How these Christians love one another!"

Jesus' way of life is the way of love. This virtue is the distinguishing feature of the follower of Christ. It should not be necessary for a Christian to wear any kind of identifying badge. To do so is not harmful, of course, but in the final analysis the badge that is the true mark of the Christian is his attitude of love.

Miriam

And Pharaoh's daughter said to her, "Go." So the girl went
and called the child's mother. —EXODUS 2:8

❧ It seems that Miriam was always older than her years.
Perhaps that was because she was the oldest child of a slave
family. Her childhood was not particularly happy. The
Egyptian overlords worked her and her parents without
mercy. Just when the king decreed that all male slave children must be killed, a baby brother came into the home.
Pharaoh did not want the male slaves to outnumber the male
Egyptians. Miriam, no doubt, helped her mother find a hiding place among the rushes of the Nile river. There they
placed the basket containing the infant Moses. It was Miriam's assignment to watch that basket with its precious con-
tents while the mother worked.

One day the princess came with her retinue to bathe in
the river and they found the hiding place. Miriam's heart
beat so loudly that she could hear it herself as she edged her
way into the group that eagerly looked into the basket. The
baby, not suspecting its danger, smiled into the face of the
princess and completely captivated her. Pharaoh's edict had
not destroyed the mother instinct in the princess' heart.

Miriam could hardly contain her joy when she saw the
princess pick up her brother and cuddle him fondly in her
arms. This was Miriam's opportune moment! She had the
courage to tell the princess that she could find a nurse who
would care for the child if she wanted to keep him. When
the princess consented Miriam brought the child's mother.
Though Miriam was shrewd beyond her years, she could not
have known that she was saving the life of one who was

destined to free his people.

But before that happened many long years intervened. She saw her brother grow into manhood and become a leading figure at the court. He could not associate freely with his people, but he was aware of their plight and became determined to help them.

Miriam never married. Since she had no children of her own, she mothered the people of her nationality. In secret meetings Moses probably confided to her the ideas that God placed in his heart, as well as his indignation at the treatment his people received.

At the proper time God called Moses to start his campaign to free the Israelites. It was a long and arduous campaign. At last, however, they were on their way to the promised land. After they crossed the sea and were safely on the other side, Miriam assumed her proper place with her gifted brother. She felt it was her task to bring joy into the lives of her people again. They had forgotten how to sing and to enjoy themselves. Miriam taught them how to sing and to dance, arts of a free people that they had lost during the many years of slavery.

She never attempted to assume any leadership that would conflict with her brother's aims, as sometimes happens when an older sister mothers a brother. She was wise enough to see her mission clearly, and her great contribution was that she brought joy into lives that were unhappy before. It is not hard to understand why the people loved her!

Rebekah

But I will go to my country and to my kindred, and take a wife for my son Isaac. . . . Before he had done speaking, behold, Rebekah, who was born to Bethuel the son of Milcah, the wife of Nahor, Abraham's brother, came out with her water jar upon her shoulder. —GENESIS 24:4, 15

❧ Abraham and his wife Sarah, who was a half-sister on his father's side, were blessed with one son, Isaac. This child was born to them when they were well along in years. God promised Abraham that through his descendants all the world would be blessed. It appeared to them for a long time that God had forgotten his promise. After they had given up all hope for a child, Isaac was born.

Their son grew into young manhood and from his mother and father he learned to worship the one true God. But if the world was to be blessed through his descendants it was necessary for him to be married also.

Isaac's marriage is an example of the "go-between" system that was in vogue in those days among the Hebrews. He did not go out to find the girl who would eventually be his wife. That responsibility was placed by Abraham on the most trusted servant in the household. Isaac really had little to say about the one whom he would marry.

To be certain that the girl would be worthy, the trusted servant was sent to Abraham's country where his cousins lived. Well supplied with gifts, he set forth with his men and camels on the important mission and traveled all the way into Mesopotamia. When he came to the village he was seeking, he prayed that God would help him make a wise choice. No sooner had they stopped at the well than girls from the village came to draw water. The servant especially noticed a beautiful girl, who saw him also and recognized that he was a stranger. She offered him a drink and said she would help him water the camels also. That was enough to indicate to the servant that this was the girl for whom he was searching.

He lost no time in telling his mission and when she heard the names Abraham, Sarah, and Isaac, she was eager to have him come to her home. There he met her parents and found that this beautiful, gifted girl was a cousin of Isaac, which made it so much the better according to the practices of those days. Gifts were lavished on her which indicated the wealth of the man whom she was to marry. In due time, with her retinue she made the journey to meet her husband.

It was a marriage arrangement altogether foreign to the American way of courting, but it seems to have worked out well. Isaac and Rebekah lived many years together and had two sons, Esau and Jacob, whose names are familiar today.

Rebekah was a wise woman, although according to New Testament standards she would hardly be approved for deceiving her husband as she did in his old age. But she knew that Jacob was the logical one of her two boys to receive the paternal blessing, although Esau was in line for it. Esau was an outdoor man who cared little for the priestly office. So she disguised Jacob in such a manner that the aged, blind Isaac gave him the blessing. Subsequent events in the lives of the two boys indicate that her judgment, if not her method, was good. Jacob was fitted to be the one through whose life all the world would be blessed.

Esther

I and my maids will also fast as you do. Then I will go to
the king, though it is against the law; and if I perish, I
perish.   —ESTHER 4:16

❧ A large portion of the Jewish people were transplanted
as captives into a strange land. There they were a minority
group and were at a disadvantage politically, economically,
and religiously. Majority groups usually tend to persecute
smaller groups who cannot dangerously resist them. That
was true of the Jewish people in Babylonia.

Among them was a beautiful Jewish orphan of the tribe
of Benjamin who had been adopted by her uncle Mordecai.
He loved Esther and recognized not only her beauty but also
the nobility of her character. When it became known that
the king was looking for a wife who would be his queen,
Mordecai saw to it through his connections at the court that
the king became acquainted with her. That was all that was
necessary. It must have been a case of love at first sight.
Although the king did not give any evidence that he knew
she was a Jew, if that would have made any difference, he
married her and he was a fortunate man to get such a beautiful and talented queen.

Sometimes when people of lowly means become affluent
they try to forget their lowly origin and disassociate themselves from their former friends. Even though Esther was
the queen of the land she kept in contact with her people
and had their interests constantly in mind.

Through jealousy in the court on the part of a high official named Haman, the king was misinformed about his
Jewish subjects. Haman was a man without principles when

it came to getting something for himself. Since Mordecai stood in his way, he influenced the king to punish the Jews with a massacre. Information about this plot was brought to Esther and it disturbed her. She had the love and loyalty of her maids at court, so she enlisted their interest also—this plot must be stopped. In the meantime Haman was so sure of his success that he had a gallows erected in the courtyard where he intended personally to supervise the hanging of Mordecai.

Esther asked her friends to fast and to pray for her. She had made up her mind to see the king and plead the cause of her people. It must be understood that even the queen did not go into the presence of the king without his bidding and it was a dangerous thing for her to do.

It was a tense moment when the king saw her there. The pleading in her eyes was more than he could resist; so he invited her to state her cause. She did it with eloquence and sincerity, while Mordecai fumed. Once the king was apprised of the facts, he reversed his former decision. Instead of Mordecai, Haman was hanged on the gallows he had erected in the courtyard.

Esther has always been remembered because of her courage and her loyalty to her people. Through her efforts they were saved, and their honesty as well as their industry were recognized and rewarded by the king.

Ruth

> But Ruth said, "Entreat me not to leave you or to return from following you; for where you go I will go, and where you lodge I will lodge; your people shall be my people, and your God my God. —RUTH 1:16

✍ We would expect these words to be spoken by a bride to her husband, as an expression of connubial loyalty. The husband is usually the breadwinner, and the bride is willing to go with him wherever he has employment. We also know by experience that when a woman marries a man she marries his family too.

But the sentiment of this text was expressed by a daughter-in-law to her mother-in-law. Naomi, the mother-in-law, had two sons. The one had married Ruth and the other, Orpah. During a famine both the sons and the father died; the three women were all widowed. Naomi decided that the wise thing for her was to return to her people. The decision meant parting with her daughters-in-law. There was no coercion or persuasion on her part; they could remain where they lived if they so desired. Orpah did choose to remain in this land where they were, among her own people. Ruth chose to go with her mother-in-law.

The book of Ruth is the only romance I know that is built around the love of a daughter-in-law for her mother-in-law. Mothers-in-law are often maligned by thoughtless people, but the truth is that many mothers-in-law are sincerely and deservedly loved by their in-law sons and daughters. The fact that some of them interfere with the happiness of their married children is no excuse for speaking disparagingly about all of them.

Naomi certainly deserved the love and devotion of Ruth.

77

After they returned to Naomi's homeland again, she was instrumental in sending Ruth to glean in the fields of the wealthy bachelor, Boaz, who was also one of her relatives. Naomi did not try to dominate her and to keep her for herself. She was sincerely interested in the girl's welfare, and was willing to give her to another if that meant happiness for Ruth.

Boaz noticed Ruth. She must have been beautiful, and with her beauty she possessed poise and a rare modesty. The discerning eye of Boaz soon picked her out among the poor people who came to his fields to glean after the harvesters. That was the beginning of a romance between Ruth and Boaz that culminated in many years of wedded happiness.

Ruth was a Moabite, not a Jew, but through her marriage with Boaz she became one of the ancestors of our Lord. In the first chapter of Matthew, verse five, we are told that Boaz and Ruth were the parents of Obed. In the lineage given in that chapter, she is the only Gentile among the forebears of the husband of Mary, mother of Jesus. .

Demas

Luke the beloved physician and Demas greet you. For Demas, in love with this present world, has deserted me and gone to Thessalonica.

—COLOSSIANS 4:14; 2 TIMOTHY 4:10

❧ There was once a small-town church in a midwestern state where the pastor conducted a series of revival services each year just before Easter. Usually on one of the evenings Old Clem would come to the altar and pray his way through to victory. From that time on until Memorial Day he led an exemplary life. On that holiday, however, the war veterans of the community usually sponsored a parade. Old Clem was a veteran too, and he was getting along in years. It was a sad sight each year to see him stagger along far behind the others; he could stay away from liquor only from Easter to May 30. Of course, we have gained more understanding of the craving for liquor in recent years, and perhaps Old Clem could be helped now, that is, if he wanted to help himself.

In a few verses the New Testament tells the story of a young man named Demas who somewhere along the way came under the influence of Paul's preaching. For a time a new light shone in his life and this young man found a noble purpose to which he dedicated himself. Thus he knew a marvelous joy. In gratitude he became a companion of Paul and was with him in Rome during the great missionary's first imprisonment. Paul sent greetings from him in some of the letters that he wrote.

In the big city, Demas must have fallen in with the wrong crowd. Perhaps he met just one stranger and these two became companions. It often happens that way. This fellow did not share Demas' convictions and convinced Demas that he was missing a lot of fun because he did not participate in the practices of the pagans.

Demas considered the pull of both sides, but he let temptation have its way. He found himself doing things that he knew Paul would not approve, and rather than change his way or face criticism, he left the fellowship of the Christians. When that happened, this young man threw away his opportunity and the Scriptures lost sight of him. The last thing Paul wrote about him, with a heavy heart, was, "Demas, in love with this present world, has deserted me."

Did Demas ever recapture the joy that he traded for temporary pleasure? Or did he spend the later years of his life sadly recalling a youthful experience that he knew he could never have again? We have no way of answering these questions.

There are many people who delight in recalling a lofty experience that they once had and can never have again. The truly Christian life, however, is a fellowship with God that only begins with conversion and that continues to grow richer, more joyful, and more beautiful with the years.

Barnabas

> News of this came to the ears of the church in Jerusalem, and they sent Barnabas to Antioch . . . for he was a good man, full of the Holy Spirit and of faith. And a large company was added to the Lord.　　—ACTS 11:22, 24

◄§ Barnabas was a Jew and a Levite, born and reared on the island of Cyprus. John Mark's mother was Barnabas' aunt. When he attained young manhood he came to Jerusalem, probably for a visit, and then decided to make his home there. The Scriptures do not reveal what his occupation was, but he must have been well situated financially until he sold his property and gave the money for the care of needy Christians in Jerusalem.

He may have met the Master personally through his aunt,

though the Bible does not mention it. He did become an influential and highly respected member of the Christian fellowship very early. By the time Paul was ready to join the fellowship, Barnabas was already regarded as a leader, and he is the one to whom Paul turned for help. If Barnabas had done nothing other than assume responsibility for Paul's conduct when he introduced him to the congregation, he should be remembered with gratitude.

Barnabas was a large man with a big heart. His original name was Joses, but after the apostles became thoroughly acquainted with him they gave him the name Barnabas, which means "son of exhortation."

When Christians fled to Antioch in the north and organized a little congregation there, the church at Jerusalem wanted to send some one to help them. But who would go to that heathen city, with its struggling congregation? It was not an easy decision for Barnabas to make, especially since he was a Jew and Antioch was largely Gentile. But he could be relied on in an emergency and he volunteered to go. Once having arrived in Antioch he saw its unlimited possibilities. Since the field was so large he felt that he needed help. The first one of whom he thought was Paul, who had returned to Tarsus. So Barnabas invited Paul to join him and gave this great apostle his first opportunity for Christian service.

The people of Antioch unintentionally paid Barnabas a wonderful compliment when they called the believers Christians. Until that time they had been known as Followers of the Way, but Barnabas made the name of Christ so well known that he and his companions were nicknamed with the name they spoke so often. Of course, "Christian" was applied at first in derision, but it has become a proud name that followers of Jesus prefer above all others.

An incident that reveals the understanding of this great man is connected with John Mark. When Paul and Barnabas planned their second missionary journey, Paul refused to take Mark along because the young man had turned back the first time. Much as Barnabas would have wished to go with Paul, he denied himself that privilege so that he could give Mark another opportunity to prove his worth.

Some biblical scholars believe that Barnabas is the writer of the letter to the Hebrews in the New Testament. Early church fathers ascribe it to him. Tradition also says that in his later years he returned to Cyprus, the place of his birth, where he did Christian work and suffered martyrdom. His remains are said to have been discovered there during the reign of the Emperor Zeno (474-491 A.D.).

Paul

> So Paul stood up, and motioning with his hand said: "Men of Israel, and you that fear God, listen." —ACTS 13:16

Outside the immediate circle of the apostles no other person did more to spread the gospel and to influence Christian thinking than did the Apostle Paul. He is called an apostle because the Lord appeared to him on the way to Damascus and called him into his service. He refers to himself as an apostle born out of season.

Paul was reared in Tarsus, a Roman city, where his father was a Roman citizen; and having been born there, Paul also was Roman. His education was the best available in those days; he was even privileged to study under Gamaliel, regarded as one of the greatest Hebrew rabbis. It was Paul's ambition to become a Pharisee, a teacher and observer of the law, and in this he succeeded. Influenced by some of his colleagues and impelled by his own zeal for the law, he undertook to do everything he could to stamp out the growing Christian religion. No doubt he studied it and found out all he could about it, so that he was well informed about this sect that he was bent on eradicating.

Then it happened on the way to Damascus, where he intended to persecute Christians who had fled there for safety. In the brightness of a flash that blinded him, the Lord appeared. It may be that even before this Paul had wondered in his heart if he was doing the right thing in persecuting these people. As was later revealed in his writings, he was fundamentally a kind man who loved his fellowmen. The teaching of Gamaliel, that if this religion was of God no one could stamp it out and if it was not of God it would die of its own accord, must have made an impression on him also. At any rate, he yielded to the call of Christ, and completely reversed his position. It took three years for Paul to readjust his thinking in the light of the gospel, and then he was ready to link himself with the Christians and to devote his great talents to the cause of Christ.

The Christians did not readily accept him when he returned to Jerusalem; it took quite some time until Barnabas vouched for his sincerity and he was received. Paul showed no resentment because of this hesitancy; he knew he had earned it by his previous actions.

The conversion of Paul is one of the most important incidents in the history of the Church, for he succeeded in establishing Christian congregations in all the major cities of the Roman empire during his lifetime. More than that, through his writings he, more than any other, interpreted the message of Jesus. There are more of his epistles in the New Testament than of any other apostolic writer.

The Gentiles became his chief interest, and that is understandable because he was a Roman citizen himself. It is largely due to his influence that the gospel spread westward into Europe and became a mighty influence in western civilization. If he had chosen to travel southward or eastward instead, the trend of the development of the Christian Church would probably have been in those directions. So the people of the western world especially owe this man a debt of gratitude.

Luke

Luke the beloved physician and Demas greet you.
—COLOSSIANS 4:14

◆§ The name Luke is so well known that he is generally regarded as one of the apostles. While he was not of that select group it is probable that he was one of the seventy disciples who knew the Master and was thus intimately connected with his ministry. He may have been the "other disciple" to whom the risen Lord revealed himself that first Easter Sunday evening on the way to Emmaus. Luke records the incident and mentions Cleophas, one of the two, by name. Since he is the writer of the narrative he could very well have been the unnamed one.

Luke was a Gentile, born in Antioch, where he received his education. He is called a physician in the sacred record. It may have been the Lord's miracles of healing that first attracted this gifted man to him; a common interest of both was the alleviation of suffering. Luke was careful to record many instances of healing on the part of Jesus, and in Acts he described the healing activities of the apostles also. But that was not his primary reason for writing his Gospel.

As a Gentile he was interested in his own people. Matthew and John were of Jewish extraction, as was also Mark. Luke wrote for Gentile readers, to convince them that Jesus was not only the Messiah of the Jewish people but also the Savior of the Gentiles.

Being a keen observer and a master of language, he described certain scenes in the Lord's life better than the other writers: the story of the birth of Jesus, for instance, and the visit of the shepherds and the wise men.

Luke became the personal physician of the Apostle Paul and accompanied him on his journeys. The activities of the apostles were of great interest to him, as well as the manner in which the Church grew in membership and strength. So he took upon himself the task of recording all of these activities. The record is known as Acts of the Apostles.

He accompanied Paul to Rome and for a time was the only one of this missionary's friends who was with him. That must have been during Paul's second imprisonment, when he sent his letter to Timothy with Tychicus. Perhaps Luke was writing Acts at that time and concluded it before Paul's second trial, because he did not record Paul's death.

What Luke did after the passing of his friend is not

known, neither do we have information concerning his death. We are in no doubt, however, about the kind of man that Luke, the beloved physician, was, nor about the complete dedication of his extraordinary talents and skills to the cause of Christ.

Mark

Get Mark and bring him with you.   —2 TIMOTHY 4:11

⋖§ John Mark was a young man, probably in his late teens when Jesus was crucified. His mother was one of the Seventy who believed in the Lord and she opened her home for the use of Jesus and his disciples. Through these contacts John Mark became acquainted with the Master. Tradition identifies him as the young man who was in the Garden of Gethsemane on the night of the betrayal. The Scriptures say that one of the officers tried to hold this young man, but he deftly slipped out of his garment and ran away naked, leaving the soldier holding the empty tunic.

John Mark is also considered to be the one who carried a pitcher of water as identification and led the two disciples to the secret upper room where they prepared the last meal that Jesus had with his disciples. Thereafter this young man figured prominently in the early Christian story.

Barnabas, a cousin, was also devoted to the gospel and a close friend of Paul. When Barnabas and Paul decided to go on a missionary tour John Mark wanted to accompany them and they took him along. But something happened to John

Mark. Perhaps he became homesick. He begged to return to Jerusalem and Paul and Barnabas continued their journey without him.

The two missionaries returned and reported the success of their work to the congregation at Jerusalem. Then they were ready to start another journey. John Mark asked to go along again. Paul refused because he had turned back the first time. Barnabas, however, wished to take him. It was decided that Paul and Silas should go together, and Barnabas could take John Mark with him. Now more mature and experienced, this young man made a significant contribution to the cause when he was given a second chance.

John Mark is best known, however, because he wrote the Gospel that bears his name. Through his close association with the apostles, especially Peter, he heard from their lips the details about the events in the life of Jesus. The writings of Mark may be regarded as those of Peter also, because it was from him that John Mark received much of his information. This Gospel was written about the year 70 A.D.

Paul thought so highly of Mark that he requested his presence with him in Rome when he was in prison. In his second letter to Timothy he asked him to bring Mark to Rome. This is the last reference to Mark in the Scriptures.

A wealth of legend and tradition has followed this great soldier of the cross. The most credible of these indicates that he became a missionary who traveled into Egypt and became the bishop of the church in the great city of Alexandria. Here he lived out a normal life span serving his Lord in the spreading of the gospel.

Timothy

To Timothy, my true child in the faith: Grace, mercy, and
peace from God the Father and Christ Jesus our Lord.

—I TIMOTHY 1:2

᯽ Paul was so close to Timothy that he referred to him as
his "true child in the faith." This is an indication that in his
youth he was converted through the preaching of Paul. Timothy's ability was recognized by Paul and under his experienced tutelage this young man became one of the great
leaders of the Church.

Timothy's mother Eunice was a Jew who was converted
to the Christian religion, as was also his grandmother Lois.
It is believed that his father was of Greek origin; that may
account for the Greek name Timothy. He was probably not
a Christian. Paul would have mentioned that when he referred to the religion of Timothy's mother and grandmother.

There are some biblical scholars who identify Timothy
with the young man who went to sleep and fell out of a
window while Paul was preaching, but that identification is
only a surmise.

Timothy and Paul became close friends, and Paul wrote
him two letters that are preserved in the New Testament.
Evidently some years later Timothy became a leader in the
congregation at Ephesus. Paul must have been traveling in
that direction from Rome after his first imprisonment. If he
intended to spend some time with Timothy he was disappointed, for he was arrested again before he arrived, most
likely at Troas, a port of Asia Minor.

The arresting officers did not show the aged missionary
much courtesy. They took him away so quickly that he did

not have time to gather his few personal belongings. While he was in prison for the second time awaiting trial he wrote to Timothy the letter from which the text is taken.

In this letter Paul indicated that he was aware of his impending danger. He said that he was ready to be offered, he had fought a good fight, he had kept the faith. But he did want to see Timothy and asked him to come to Rome; he assured him that the congregation at Ephesus would not be without a leader because Paul was sending Tychicus with his letter. There is a warm personal touch in his request that Timothy stop at Troas on the way to Rome and bring his cloak that was left in the home of Carpus, and his books also.

Whether Timothy arrived in Rome before Paul's execution is not known. Early writers say that he returned to Ephesus where he was the leader of the church for many years. The heathen observances of the Ephesians ran into gross excesses and on one occasion when Timothy rebuked them for their sins at a celebration they stoned him. He died three days later and was laid to rest in Ephesus by the people of the church who loved and respected him.

James, Brother of the Lord

Is not this the carpenter, the son of Mary and brother of James?   —MARK 6:3

◄§ This James, the son of Joseph and Mary, was born after Jesus. There are a number of references to him in the New

Testament, and it is believed by some that although he was not one of the Twelve he did belong to the Seventy. Other scholars say that James did not confess faith in the Lord until after the ascension. The latter view may be more probable because on the cross Jesus commended his mother to the care of John. If James had given evidence of his faith before that time, Jesus might have given Mary into the care of her own flesh and blood.

It may have been difficult for James to reconcile the Master's lofty claims with their common, everyday life together in the home. Then when he saw the great love and patience of Jesus on the cross, the manifestations at Pentecost, and the appearances of the Lord after his crucifixion, he was ready also to confess his faith.

James became a sincere worker in the Church. His ability was recognized by the believers and he became respected as one of their leaders together with Peter and John. Like Paul, he held that Gentiles could be received into the Church. He advocated, as Peter did, that Jewish Christians should continue to observe the law as they had been taught, and that Gentile Christians should hold the law in respect.

The Epistle of James in the New Testament was probably written toward the close of his life when the Christian way had lost some of its first fresh vigor. It is addressed especially to Jewish Christians. It contains many passages that recall the sayings of Jesus, particularly those of the Sermon on the Mount. Its use in the Church was widespread, and it is chiefly responsible for the emphasis of the apostolic Church on the rite of anointing the sick with oil. This rite later developed into the sacrament of extreme unction in the Roman Catholic Church and is used as a healing ritual in some Protestant denominations today.

The Epistle of James also emphasizes the importance of Christian service to orphans and widows, and thus also to the underprivileged. As the head of the Christian community at Jerusalem James felt that the compassion of the Lord should be practiced by his followers.

A variety of legend grew around this brother of Jesus. It is said that he was nicknamed "Camel-knees" because he developed calluses on his knees through frequent prayer. Concerning his death there are two accounts. One reports that he was thrown from a tower by some Pharisees. The other account, by the historian Josephus, is that a party of Sadducees caused him to be stoned to death.

Salome

> There were also women looking on from afar, among whom were Mary Magdalene, and Mary the mother of James the younger and of Joses, and Salome. —MARK 15:40

◄§ Beneath the cross on Calvary Salome's hopes for the kingdom may have been shattered, but nothing could destroy her love for the Lord. With a few other faithful ones she faced the shame of the mob on the hill that day because she was loyal and loved much.

Salome had not always been like that. At one time she was self-seeking and ambitious. Her husband, Zebedee, was an honest, hard-working fisherman who was successful enough in his business to have hired servants. Because of his economic status their home was better than the average. She and Zebedee were proud of their two sons. They grew into fine young men who worked with their father.

It may have been through her boys, James and John, that Salome first learned to know the Lord. After they became his followers she opened her home on many occasions to entertain Jesus and his disciples. Thus she learned to know Jesus well and became convinced that he was the Messiah for whom she and her people had long been praying.

During the period when Jesus was popular she felt that his kingdom would be established on the earth with a worldly form of government. In that event she wanted her two boys to have important positions. No doubt Salome thought about this for some time before she decided to settle the matter by talking with Jesus about it. She tried to persuade Jesus to give the most honored positions, one to James and the other to John. In the kindest way that he knew Jesus answered her request by telling her that if they proved worthy of this responsibility they would have it. In other words, he indicated that important positions in his kingdom would go to those who deserved them. Neither political pull nor personal friendship could be the decisive consideration. And Salome accepted his explanation because he helped her to understand.

There are those who believe her two sons inherited their determination from her. Whether they received it from her or not, they certainly used it to good purpose in the Master's work.

Salome was so loyal that she willingly faced the disgrace of Calvary that dark day when her Lord was crucified. Then on the first Easter morning she was with the small group of faithful women who went to the tomb because they wanted to perform the last rites of love. It was there that her sorrow was turned into joy by the good news that Jesus was not dead, but alive. At last she felt that her hopes had not been in vain.

How Salome served the Christian cause later in life is not known, but it can be said with assurance that she continued to offer her home to believers as a meeting place and as a haven of hospitality. Through her life she must have led many to become followers of the Way.

*P*hoebe

> I commend to you our sister Phoebe, a deaconess of the church at Cenchreae, that you may receive her in the Lord as befits the saints, and help her in whatever she may require from you, for she has been a helper of many and of myself as well. —ROMANS 16:1, 2

◄§ Phoebe was aptly named. The word means "shining," and she was surely a comforting light to many people. By the time Paul wrote his letter to the Romans she was well known among the Christians and she planned to visit the congregation in Rome.

In the apostolic Church deacons were chosen by the congregation to assist the apostles and other leaders so that they could devote themselves more completely to spiritual work. At first only men were deacons but it was not long until some women felt called by God to devote their lives to such service. The very first of these women mentioned in the New Testament was Phoebe. Her duties as a deaconess were many: she prepared women and girls for baptism; she saw to it that the place of worship was clean and in order; sometimes she prepared the elements for holy communion and baptism; but most of all she visited the sick and the poor, helped where she could, and called the attention of the congregation to the needs of the suffering.

The deaconess made such a significant contribution to the religious life of the fellowship that the office came to be regarded as permanently necessary. By the third and fourth centuries it was fully recognized and there was an official form for the consecration of the deaconess. The consecrating officer was the bishop.

There were many deaconesses in the early history of the Church. Partly through their influence institutions were established for the care of the poor and the sick. These institutions were the ancestors of the modern hospital. The deaconess did not hesitate to do the most menial tasks in the alleviation of suffering and pain. Some who were wealthy used their homes as institutions and devoted all their resources to that humanitarian work.

As the centuries passed the deaconess order died out. It was replaced by male nursing orders, and later by nursing orders and sisterhoods in the Roman Catholic Church. For about 150 years after the time of the Reformation no nursing orders appeared in Protestant churches. Luther saw the need but never got around to establishing them. In the early 1800's the diaconate was revived in the Protestant churches of Germany. From Germany it spread to other countries, including the United States.

The revival of the order of the deaconess kindled a new interest in healing in the Protestant Church. Many Protestant hospitals were started that have grown into large institutions today. While a number of denominations have deaconesses who nurse the sick and care for the poor, the complaint common with all of them is that there are not enough young women willing to devote their lives to this work of compassion. Unless the number of volunteers can be increased, it may be that the order started by Phoebe will again vanish from the scene of Christian service.

Marcella

> He said also to the man who had invited him, "When you give a dinner or a banquet, do not invite your friends or your brothers or your kinsman or rich neighbors, lest they also invite you in return, and you be repaid. But when you give a feast, invite the poor, the maimed, the lame, the blind, and you will be blessed, because they cannot repay you. You will be repaid at the resurrection of the just."
>
> —LUKE 14:12-14

⋖ Wealth may be used to promote the kingdom of God. Jesus said that the love of money is spiritually detrimental, not money itself. When it is used constructively it can be helpful not only to the one who has it but to others who are benefited.

In the church at Rome there were a number of wealthy young matrons who used their possessions in the service of God and their fellowmen. Marcella was one of these.

Born in an aristocratic family, she married when she was quite young in the light of modern standards. When she was widowed after only seven months of marriage she was heartbroken. Through devotion to the memory of her husband and to the Lord, she vowed not to marry again but to devote the remainder of her life to Christian service and charity.

In order to be sure that her relatives were treated in a fair way, she turned over to them more than their just share of her wealth. The rest she kept to use in helping the poor and the afflicted. Since she came of a noble family, she was well educated, and when Jerome came to Rome in the year 382 she became acquainted with him, as did her friend, Paula.

Soon thereafter she converted her palatial home on the Aventine way into a place where Christian women could come to live, study, and pray until they were sufficiently motivated by the spirit of Christ to go as ministering servants to the poor and the afflicted. Many wealthy widows who were once very haughty came there for a season, and then found themselves giving their time and money to improve the conditions of the unfortunate and the sick.

Marcella became well versed in Christian doctrine and made a journey to the Holy Land with Paula. On the way they visited with the scholarly Jerome in Antioch. Paula remained in Jerusalem and Bethlehem, but Marcella returned to her home in Rome. Here she continued to give her life in Christian service. Her love for God and man filled the place made vacant in her heart at the death of her husband and she found happiness and peace again.

When the horde of pagan Goths captured Rome in 410 A.D. Marcella was taken prisoner. Somehow they found out that she had been wealthy and they took for granted that she still was. When she told them that she did not have money they tortured her unmercifully to get her to reveal where she had hidden her supposed wealth. As a result of this heartless treatment she died shortly thereafter. Undoubtedly the words of the Lord applied to her life: "And you will be blessed, because they cannot repay you. You will be repaid at the resurrection of the just."

$Paula$

He who is faithful in a very little is faithful also in much.
—LUKE 16:10

✑ Paula was one of the Roman matrons in the early Christian Church who excelled in the devotion with which they consecrated their lives and their wealth. Born at Rome in the year 347, she was the child of a wealthy family who took great pride in tracing its ancestry, which included a queen and a king. Because she was reared in aristocratic surroundings she was expected by her family to marry a man whose genealogy was no less impressive than her own. In addition to her family connections she was a beautiful girl, and when she reached adolescent years she married a very important person, a senator named Toxotius.

Paula was converted to the Christian way. Her husband died in 380. Two years after his death the Church had an important meeting in Rome and Paula invited two of the dignitaries to lodge in her home. These great Christian guests made a profound impression on Paula, and she decided at that time to devote the rest of her life and her wealth to the work of the Church.

Two years after she made the decision one of her daughters died. Like Naomi, she felt that she was resting under the shadow of God's hand, and especially so when a second daughter died also. Her youngest child, Blaesilla, was about to be married; and since her son had already established his home she believed the time had come for her to give herself completely to the Lord's work.

With a friend, Marcella, she planned to go to Antioch in Asia Minor where the scholarly Jerome was at work translating the Scriptures into the current Latin language. The children tried in vain to dissuade her from her purpose. Being proficient in languages, especially Hebrew, she desired to help the great scholar in his important task.

With her friend, she made the journey. She had the great satisfaction of working with Jerome in translating the prophets. From Antioch she went to the Holy Land, where she used much of her wealth in building and maintaining hospitals for the sick and inns for travelers. In many instances a hospital and an inn were combined into one institution. Sick people of every description were given Christian care. Paula assisted with the nursing; she considered no service too humble for her to render in the name of Christ. These institutions of benevolence were the predecessors of the modern church-related hospitals, homes for children, and homes for the aged.

Paula died at Bethlehem in the year 404. Bishops from the surrounding area and many common people came to the funeral service. Their demonstration of love gave evidence of the high esteem in which they held this consecrated servant of God. They accorded her the highest honor when they placed her remains in the cave of the nativity where, according to tradition, Christ was born.

Alexander, the Physician

Blessed are you when men revile you and persecute you and utter all kinds of evil against you falsely on my account.

—MATTHEW 5:11

◆§ When Jesus spoke the words of this beatitude he knew that the time was near when his followers would face ridicule and persecution. Shortly after his ascension the political and religious authorities began their attempt to abolish the new faith. Because it taught virtues which the authorities regarded with disfavor, they were determined to exterminate it. As the years passed, hatred toward the Christians grew ever more intense.

Disregarding the risk involved, many people confessed faith in Jesus, and the Church continued to grow in the face of opposition. Among the early converts was a physician named Alexander. Whether the knowledge that Luke was a physician made him receptive to the gospel is not known, but he chose to confess faith in the Lord and to accept the Christian way of life.

Alexander saw many of his Christian associates arrested and taken to prison. The prisoners were permitted to have visitors. This concession may appear on the surface to have been humane, but the civil authorities had a sinister purpose in this feigned generosity. They carefully observed who came to call on the prisoners. In that way they learned to know many other Christians and later they arrested them also.

Physicians were needed to minister to the sick Christian prisoners but none of the pagan doctors would wait upon them, fearing that they would also be identified with the believers. Alexander volunteered his services although he knew that it meant exposing himself to arrest. He was not afraid to endanger his own life if he could help his brethren in the faith by doing it.

The following incident occurred in what is now the city of Lyons in southern France, during the second century. Hatred toward the Christians grew out of bounds and one Sunday a mob descended on the little congregation that had assembled for worship. With hootings and vicious blows members of the church were dragged to the public forum where the magistrates of the city ordered them to be imprisoned until the governor would arrive to try their cases. Many of those imprisoned were seriously injured and were in desperate need of medical care. Alexander bravely went into the prison and dressed their wounds. The authorities observed him there and he was arrested while in the act of binding a wound.

The governor finally arrived, and instead of giving them a fair trial all he did was to ask each prisoner if he was a Christian. Those who answered in the affirmative were sentenced to death. Alexander was brought forth also and in plain words professed his acceptance of Jesus Christ as his Savior. With others whose wounds he had bound the physician was condemned to death in the year 177. His life is a memorial to the kind of courage and compassion that move the Christian to answer the call of human need, whatever the cost.

Ephraem, the Syrian

Let not loyalty and faithfulness forsake you; bind them
about your neck. —PROVERBS 3:3

In the first centuries of our Christian era there were
some followers of Christ who felt impelled to withdraw
entirely from society. They believed that there was so much
sin in the world that they could save their own souls better
by having no contacts with other people.

Strange as it may seem, the first hospital devoted exclu-
sively to the care of the sick was temporarily established by
one of these recluses. His name was Ephraem and his ac-
quaintances called him "the Syrian." Withdrawing from
the world, he forgot comforts and conveniences while his
waking hours were devoted to thoughts about Jesus.

About 350 A.D. Ephraem lived near the city of Edessa
in Asia Minor. Then a plague spread among the people of
the city soon after they had managed to withstand the
ravages of a famine. Since many of the residents were undernourished, the disease spread rapidly and caused great distress. Ephraem heard about the sad situation from a visitor
who happened to come upon his secluded hut. The tale of
woe moved him strangely and he decided to go into the
city. Once he was there, he saw the misery and the neglect;
and it did not take him long to make a decision. He forgot
about being a hermit, visited the people in Edessa who still
had financial resources, and shamed them for their selfish-
ness and lack of compassion—for permitting so many poor
people to die in hunger and unattended. Profoundly touched
by his plea, many of them told him that they would provide
what was needed by the sick if some one could be found to

nurse them. Ephraem assured them that he would provide the nursing care—what he needed was money.

Many of the wealthier people accepted his challenge. With their gifts he bought 300 beds and placed them in a large public building. Stricken people were brought there until the beds were filled. City officials were afraid to come near the place, so there was no interference on the part of the authorities.

Then he appealed to Christian men and women to help him care for the sick and many were brave enough to volunteer. Ephraem was there day and night, and although he had no professional training in that work, through his compassion and common sense many lives were saved. The incident also impressed upon the wealthier people their responsibility for the welfare of the poor and the underprivileged.

Unfortunately Ephraem, the Syrian, did not devote his life to works of compassion. As soon as the epidemic subsided the old urge to seclusion came over him again. Quietly he left the city to return to his lowly hut and to sever all contacts with the people. Nothing more is known about him, except that he died in seclusion a few years later. He was a man who recognized a great need in the time of emergency and was willing to overlook his personal desires until the need was met. After the emergency his own spiritual security became again the overmastering impulse of his life.

When Things Go Wrong

I hope to see you in passing as I go to Spain.

—ROMANS 15:24

◄§ Did you ever make plans to do something you felt was very important, and at the last minute something came up that prevented you from doing it and you had to change your plans? Psychologists tell us that intelligence is the ability to adjust to new situations. When a person must change plans hurriedly or find a substitute for something he has long wanted to do, an adjustment is necessary.

The Apostle Paul experienced that also. He wrote to the congregation in Rome that he intended to visit them when he made his journey into Spain. Paul longed to go to that country which was on the very fringe of civilization in his time. He had already planted the seeds of the gospel in the great cities of the other countries bordering the Mediterranean. The name "Spain" meant new adventure.

Paul made big plans. But as far as we know he was never permitted to make that journey. Events took place in his life that altered his cherished plans; he was arrested, and taken as prisoner to Rome. Instead of arriving as an honored guest, he was brought into the city under arrest. He could not even visit the congregation, and those who wanted to see him had to come to the place where he was held as a prisoner. Instead of going on into Spain, he had to be content with preaching the gospel to a small circle of friends and visitors. And certainly he made the most of his opportunities, circumscribed as they were. Here in prison he also had time to write some of the letters which later became part of our New Testament.

We are told that daydreaming is harmful, although its evil effects have never been explained to me in a convincing way. Perhaps that is because I confuse making plans with daydreaming. I doubt if there is any ambitious person who does not make plans for the future. Among those plans may be the one great thing a person desires to do.

And then it happens! Something comes into life that prevents the accomplishment of that dream. It may be sickness, financial loss, the death of a loved one, or an accident. Instead of getting into Spain we find ourselves permanently stranded in Rome. That is when we need intelligence and spiritual fortitude to make the best of a new situation.

We can do three things in this dilemma. The first is to rebel against the circumstance and keep on dreaming that some day we will get to Spain. The second is to become bitter and complain about our misfortune. The third is to let God use us where we are. There are opportunities in Rome also, probably better than those in Spain, and we find satisfaction and peace in doing our best wherever we are. I believe the last adjustment will bring the most enduring satisfaction.

A Blank Bible

So shall my word be that goes forth from my mouth; it shall not return to me empty. —ISAIAH 55:11

A friend handed me what appeared to be a nice morocco-bound Bible. The words "Holy Bible" were engraved on it in gold. He said, "There, look at this, tell me what you think of it." I thought it strange that he would hand me a Bible with that request, so I opened it to the title page and noticed that it was a King James version with the usual dedication. As I was about to hand it back he urged, "Go on, look at it some more." I turned the page and to my amazement it was blank, as were all the rest of the pages!

The blank Bible was an unusual printer's error. My friend ordered a Bible by mail and that is what he got. He noticed my amazement and made the thought-provoking remark, "What if all Bibles were like that!"

When people are sick, the one book that is most often requested is the Bible. In it we have the great promises of God to comfort us in the time of need. Of course, sickness is not the only stress that arises in life. But for every need the Bible has a message.

There are some people who get along without the Bible and hardly miss it because they have never become acquainted with it, nor do they know what it really does for a person. Before we became accustomed to the radio we lived very well without one. That was because we were unaware of the entertainment, music, news reports, and interesting programs that the radio brings. Now, after we have become accustomed to it, if something goes wrong with our radio we miss it greatly until we get it back from the repair man. We miss it because we know what it does for us.

If the Bible were blank we would not know about the love of God. We might still be in the ignorance of fear and superstition, or be living without the peace of mind that accompanies a faith that relies upon the love of God.

If the Bible were blank, we would not know about Jesus,

our Lord. Through him we have forgiveness for our sins, salvation, and the assurance of eternal life. Those who have known these blessings for a long time realize how barren life would be without them.

If the Bible were blank, the eternal destiny of our loved ones would be a complete mystery. God gives us such assurances in the Word that we can with confidence commit the dead to God's care.

If the Bible were blank, we would not have the conviction that righteousness will ultimately triumph because the will of God is good and purposeful. This conviction gives us the courage to look ahead with confidence, and to use our powers for the benefit of man and not for his destruction.

If the Bible were blank, God, as we know him through its sacred pages, would be taken out of our lives. We can be deeply grateful that his promise is true: "It shall not return to me empty."

The Importance of Being One

So God created man in his own image.   —GENESIS 1:27

◦§ One day some students were discussing the creation of man. Evidently they were rather disgusted with the way some men act because they were trying to fathom the reason why God created man in the first place. One of them took a book of philosophy from the shelf, turned to a certain page, and read an involved interpretation of the creation by an ancient philosopher. When he finished reading, one student asked, "What is he trying to say?" Another replied, "I think he is trying to say that God created man because he was lonely." This simple explanation caused a ripple of laughter, but when they discussed the import of the observation they came to the conclusion that the student was not so far wrong.

After God created the earth, the sun, the moon, and the stars, he made the vegetation on the earth and then the living creatures to inhabit it. When all this was finished there was not a creature that could speak to him, thank him, or love him. It was then that God created man in his own image and made him a living soul. God created man with such capability that he might know him and have fellowship with him. He endowed man with great potentialities!

There is not much in the world today that reminds man of his greatness. Certainly not his daily grind to earn a living, or the pressure that is put on an individual to produce, or the awful fact that we constantly kill each other in wars, and with automobiles and motorcycles. Human life seems to be very cheap and unimportant. The tragedy of our age is that, with our hatreds, jealousies, and prejudices, we act smaller than we really are.

But man is potentially great! The Sermon on the Mount, which is the constitution of the kingdom of God, emphasizes the importance of the individual. God thought man important enough for him to come to earth and live with him in order to show him how much God loves him and how great he can be if he so desires.

When we think small, we act small. When we think big, we act big. That is why God gave us the Bible, to help us

107

think big so that we will act like children of God, which we are.

There are so many people in the world and so many who regard life cheaply that it is rather easy to get the opinion that one person does not amount to much. But God does not think so. He gave each one a mind, a soul, and a body, a combination no other creature possesses. Each individual can be important in the sphere of his activity and his influence. With this potential greatness there is a corresponding responsibility, and as the individual realizes his responsibility he also realizes his greatness.

Even the lowliest person is important in the eyes of God because, like God, he is made to live forever. God's plan for his life reaches out beyond the brief span of years that are lived here. The important thing now is to live in such a manner that there may be some sensible reasons why life should be prolonged indefinitely.

One Talent

> To one he gave five talents, to another two, to another one, to each according to his ability. —MATTHEW 25:15

◄§ Occasionally we may be inclined to envy people who seem to have so many talents that they can do almost anything they wish. At least, it seems to us that they have many talents. Perhaps if we knew all the particulars we would find that the one person whom we especially envy is not blessed with many talents at all.

There was a young minister who learned in his seminary days that he was not a brilliant student. His mental capacity was average, while many of his classmates were in a higher mental bracket. But he wanted to be successful for the Lord in his ministry, so he studied exceptionally hard, made passing grades, and was ordained. In his first charge he found that his preaching was only average, but he was sincere. It soon became apparent that the people liked him because he was friendly and tried to be helpful wherever he could. It was amazing to him that people came to church in larger numbers than ever before in that community. Almost every member spoke approvingly about their good minister. It was not his brilliance that drew them, but his sincerity.

As in almost every graduating class, one was the "shiner" who made the best grades. He could play musical instruments and was active in the college plays. In fact, he was the most popular man on the campus and it seemed that everything came his way. When the college days were over, he also became the pastor of a congregation. Many of the members had little appreciation for his polished oratory. He stayed there two years and moved to another congregation, then in a few years to another. For some reason he just did not "click" in the ministry, and after repeated failures he decided to try his hand at a job of selling. He gave up the ministry, went into business, and became quite successful as a salesman.

The reason for his failure in the ministry was that he relied on his many talents and never developed the art of sincerity. He depended entirely on his own abilities, and his people were not long in sensing that there was something vital missing in his preaching and his teaching. He was wise in leaving the ministry and going into a profession where his talents could help him be successful. I am not suggesting that many talents are a hindrance in the ministry or any other profession, but that they cannot be an adequate substitute for sincerity.

The individual with only one talent may be as successful as the person with many, if he uses his one talent carefully and develops it. A great benefactor of our race, Charles Steinmetz, possessed neither a winning personality nor an attractive body, but he did have talent in electrical engineering. Thomas Edison, whose name is often associated with Steinmetz, was a poor student in school, came from the small town of Milan, Ohio, and did not have wealth or prestige. He had the one talent of an inventive skill, and he exploited it to the limit.

Some of the worst failures in life are five-talent people who leave God out of their lives because they think they can get along without him. The most satisfying experiences come to those who, with God's help, devote themselves to the task at hand with whatever talents they may possess. One talent is all we need if we dedicate it to God in service.

Being Thankful for Others

I thank my God in all my remembrance of you.
—PHILIPPIANS 1:3

◂§ The Apostle Paul wrote a letter to his friends in the city of Philippi. He knew them quite well because he had visited with them and preached to the small congregation there. He also had been a guest in some of their homes. He thought of them so kindly that he thanked God upon every remembrance of them.

Philippi was the first city in Greece where Paul preached the gospel, and the small group who heard him believed and confessed their faith. Among the converts was Lydia, who was a business woman, "a seller of purple." Silas was with Paul at the time. A few days later the two men were arrested and flogged for freeing a slave girl who had got herself into the clutches of a syndicate of unscrupulous men. Their friends in the congregation prayed for them and that night they were miraculously released from prison by an earthquake. The jailer himself was so impressed that he asked Paul and Silas what he must do to be saved. The next morning the two prisoners were officially released by the magistrate, who realized he had made a mistake by arresting and beating them. Then Paul and Silas were invited to the home of Lydia where they rested until their wounds were healed.

On one occasion Paul appealed to the congregation to make donations of money to relieve the needs of poverty-stricken Christians in Jerusalem, and these people demonstrated their love by contributing liberally to the fund. This expression of compassion and generosity also caused Paul to value their friendship highly. When we consider the love, generosity, and friendliness of the members of the congregation at Philippi, we do not wonder that Paul always remembered them with gratitude.

Does anyone thank God when he remembers us? The answer to this question depends on the attitude of each of us individually. People who complain that they have no friends usually have no one to blame but themselves. If we are selfish and inconsiderate, how can others think of us kindly? But if we evidence love, generosity, and friendliness in our relationships with others, we may be sure that they will remember us with gratitude.

The Christ in Christmas

And when he entered Jerusalem, all the city was stirred, saying, "Who is this?"
—MATTHEW 21:10

◄§ On the first Sunday in Advent, which is the fourth before Christmas, the selection of Scripture that is generally read in church services is the 21st chapter of Matthew, verses 1 to 9. This is the story of Jesus' triumphal entry into Jerusalem. The people lined the streets and hailed him, shouting, "Hosanna to the Son of David! Blessed be he who comes in the name of the Lord!" His entry into the holy city is a symbol of the manner in which he may come into human lives and be born there anew each year.

The secular observance of Christmas has become commercialized to such an extent that it is easy for many people to forget the One whose birthday is being observed. In fact, the popular abbreviation of the word Christmas into "Xmas" leaves "Christ" out of it and this practice may be suggestive of the way in which his birthday is observed in many homes. But no matter how thoughtless some people may be, Christ cannot be pushed aside entirely. Even the "X" in Xmas is an ancient secret symbol which was used by Christians to denote their Christ.

112

"Who is this?" many people in Jerusalem asked when they heard about the stir that was made by Jesus' entry into their city. The Advent season encourages us to ask also, "Whose birthday is this that we are going to observe?" During this season the Church keeps saying to us in various ways, "It is the birthday of Christ that we are about to celebrate." If we become absorbed with our own pleasures we may overlook him altogether. The purpose of Christmas is to make the Lord happy by the manner in which we remember his great love for us. The best gift we can give him is the offering of our own devotion. With that attitude we change X-mas into Christ-mas.

It's Catching

Be kind to one another. —EPHESIANS 4:32

◄§ At a meeting of business men one began to tell the story of a family whose home had recently burned during the night. There were four children in the family, he said, and neighbors had taken them in until a house could be found for them. At this point he was interrupted by a man who asked if their furniture and clothing had been lost in the fire. The speaker said that all their belongings had been destroyed.

The man interrupted the speaker a second time. He said that he was willing to give five dollars to help that poor family, and he proceeded to give the money to the speaker. For a few moments there was silence, then one after another produced "folding money" and handed his gift to the man who related the incident. When it was all over, this surprised man, who had never thought of receiving a collection for the unfortunate family, had a considerable amount of money to give them. One man started it—kindness is catching!

Most people are fundamentally kind; some one has only to lead the way and they are glad for an opportunity to give expression to their feelings. That is one of the reasons for the almost universal observance of Christmas—it gives everyone an excuse for being kind.

Many people, especially men, are a little ashamed of being sentimental and kind. They seem to think that these emotions are an expression of weakness. Then Christmas comes each year when sentiment and kindness are accepted as being masculine. Even the toughest thirteen-year-old boy will have enough courage at this time to give his best girl a present. He wanted to do it for a long while but he was afraid of being teased. At Christmas time he can do it because everyone else whom he knows is expressing kindness and affection. Many people to whom it does not occur at other times to give a tangible expression of their feelings, will do it unashamedly at Christmas. That is because others do it—it's catching!

The spirit of kindness is in the anticipation with which people await Christmas. They love the season, not only because they receive presents but also because it gives them an opportunity to be kind to others. It is unfortunate to be so inhibited that we suppress our kindness so much of the time. Our relations with one another could be much more wholesome and pleasant if more of us had sufficient courage to be kind all the time. Try it—it's catching!

A Bouquet of Christmas Joys

And the angel said to them, Be not afraid; for behold, I bring you good news of a great joy which will come to all the people. —LUKE 2:10

There is an old allegory about two servants sent out by their king, who was also a philosopher. The one servant was instructed to bring back a basket of flowers. The other was told to fill his basket with thorns. When they returned the man who was sent to gather thorns reported first. "Well done," said the king. "I see your basket is filled with thorns, but I thought that you might bring a flower also."

"A flower!" exclaimed the servant. Then in a calmer voice he said, "I paid no attention to the flowers. I was looking for thorns."

Then the king turned to the second man and said, "Well done. I see your basket is filled with flowers, but I notice that you brought no thorns."

"No thorns?" said the man. "I was looking for roses and paid no attention to the thorns."

Undoubtedly both men worked in the same garden. The one was looking for thorns and found them. The other was so intent on gathering flowers that the thorns escaped him. Is it not true that we usually find what we are looking for?

Christmas is a season of the year when we can fill the basket of life with flowers and do it without much effort. It is an easy matter to gather a bouquet of Christmas joys, and we do not need many flowers to fill a basket.

The rose of the joy of living is one that should be in every Christmas bouquet. God's great love for us, demonstrated so vividly in the birth of the Savior, is sufficient to inspire us with joy. Christian people have reasons to be happy and to rejoice, as Paul so often admonishes. While we admire our Puritan forefathers for many things, we cannot agree with their estimate of religion as a somber thing. In Massachusetts it was illegal for many years to observe Christmas because the authorities did not want people to be happy. They thought there was special merit in being miserable. In contrast to that attitude we believe that Christmas comes once a year to give us an opportunity to enjoy living, and that is one rose we want to place in our bouquet.

Another flower is the joy of loving. The joy of loving is seen everywhere in the Savior's life. Every individual, no matter how important or unimportant, was the recipient of his love. He said, "By this all men will know that you are my disciples, if you have love for one another." Christmas is the happiest season of the year because it gives us many opportunities to express our Christian love.

The third rose for the Christmas bouquet is the joy of giving. When we were children, our greater joy at Christmas time was experienced in receiving gifts. As we grew older, while we still enjoyed receiving gifts, we found that there was even more joy in giving.

During this season of the year we have an opportunity to remember many friends to whom we are too busy to give much thought or consideration during the year. The giving of gifts and cards brings satisfaction. Then also there are many less fortunate people with whom we can share our abundance, and making them happy is a pleasure indeed.

The roses of living, of loving, and of giving are only three flowers, but they do make a beautiful bouquet of Christmas joy.

Before the Door

Behold, I stand at the door and knock; if any one hears my voice and opens the door, I will come in to him and eat with him, and he with me. —REVELATION 3:20

◄§ Doors are important to a house or any other structure. They permit access, and they may also prevent it. The main door is especially important because it indicates something about the use of the building. For instance, a very wide and high door tells us that it is intended to permit big things to pass through it. A garage must be equipped with an entrance like that. Doors on a hangar must be exceptionally large because the wings of a plane are wide.

Residence doors vary in size and pattern. Some are very pretty and inviting. Others are quite solid and forbidding. The latter type is often equipped with a small window so that those who are within can peep out and see who is there before they open it. Some doors open outward and make us step around them, while others open inward and welcome us.

A door should open easily, especially the door of a church. One Christmas Eve a midnight candlelight service was held in a church. Many people attended to celebrate the birthday of their Savior. It was so cold that it was necessary to keep the church door closed. A few days later the pastor talked with some people who had recently moved into the city and whom he had invited to the service. They told him that they came to the church that night but they were a little late and the worship had already started. For that reason they hesitated to enter, but after a few moments they decided to go in anyway. When they tried to open the door it would not budge. Evidently the ushers did not hear them. Because the visitors were strangers and timid, they returned to their home disappointed.

After the pastor heard their story he saw to it that a carpenter was engaged to make that door open easily. He did not want people to stay away from the church because it was hard to get into. Managers of business houses know that it pays to make entrance into their places of business easy. This pastor felt that the Lord's work was more important than any other and he wanted to make it inviting for people to enter.

One door is probably better known the world over than any other. It is depicted by an artist and shows Jesus knocking upon it. If we observe it closely we notice that there is no way to open that door from the outside. To permit Jesus to enter the owner will have to use the latch on the inside. The painting means that Jesus is knocking on the door of life and that the only way he can get in is for the individual to open the door of his heart. Jesus will not force his entrance on anyone who does not want him.

The Lord is always knocking on the door of life because he loves. During certain seasons of the year, especially during Lent, many become more aware of his presence. "Behold, I stand at the door and knock," he says in the book of Revelation, "if anyone hears my voice and opens the door, I will come in to him and eat with him, and he with me." He is standing before the door of our life now, knocking. If we want him to enter we need to open the door from our side and say sincerely, "Come, Lord Jesus, be thou our guest." Then the door is opened so that he can enter and we can have fellowship with him.

Love Warms Our Hearts

See what love the Father has given us, that we should be called children of God; and so we are. —1 JOHN 3:1

◄§ In his day Paganini was one of the most accomplished violinists in the whole world. His great talent was in demand everywhere, and those who heard him in concerts acclaimed his playing as the best they had ever heard.

One cold Christmas day, while he was giving concerts in England, Paganini saw a poor, blind man playing a violin on a London street, trying to earn enough money in tips to buy something to eat. The hungry fiddler played again and again with fingers stiffened from the old. Somehow his tunes failed to appeal sufficiently for him to get any alms.

Two men paused across the street and listened. Then one of them walked over to the blind player and said, "Won't the people give you any money?"

"No," was the reply, "it is too cold and they will not open their windows."

"Lend me your fiddle," the man said, "and I will play a tune for you."

The speaker placed the instrument to his chin and played a tune the like of which had never been heard and probably never would be heard on that street again. Soon windows were opened and coins were handed out to be placed in the blind man's cup. Then the player said to him, "There you are; you can go home now. You have enough to keep you for a few days at least."

The blind man never knew that the stranger who serenaded on the street that day for him was the greatest living violinist.

Our heavenly Father is the God of love, and when we know him a responsive chord is struck in our own hearts. As far as it is possible for us, we imitate him. He would have done for the poor blind fiddler just what Paganini did.

One cold winter morning the windows in the kitchen of a home were covered with frost. The little boy, up early that morning, took a knife and started to scrape on one of the windows.

His mother said, "What are you trying to do? You may break the glass doing that!"

"I want to see out of the window," was his impatient reply.

"If you will just wait a few minutes until it gets warm in here, the frost will melt," his mother told him.

When there is warmth in the heart it clears the vision so that we can see opportunities to demonstrate our love. The frost melts from the personality because the Father God has bestowed his love upon us.